The T-Series MGs

The T-Series MGs

A collector's guide
by Graham Robson

MOTOR RACING PUBLICATIONS LTD
28 Devonshire Road, Chiswick, London W4 2HD, England

ISBN 0 900549 51 3
First published 1980

Printed in Great Britain by The Garden City Press Limited,
Letchworth, Hertfordshire SG6 1JS.

Contents

Introduction

When I was asked to prepare my third book in this *Collector's Guide* series, I had no hesitation in choosing a study of the T-Series MGs. The time has now come, surely, for their true worth to be analyzed. It is, after all, more than 25 years since the last of the line — a TF1500 — was built at Abingdon, and in that time the cars' reputations have changed several times. How can it be, for instance, that when the cars were in production there was persistent criticism of their looks and their performance, but that they were then in the vanguard of increasing values of so-called 'classic cars' in the 1970s, and that they are now becoming collectors' items, to be fussed over, and entered in a concours, rather than to be enjoyed for day-to-day motoring?

As with the other volumes in this series, the book is not written to glorify a false image for the T-Series cars, or to try to destroy a fine reputation. It has been arranged to give a great deal of factual information about the T-Series MGs built between 1936 and 1955, of the works-sponsored competition programmes connected with these cars, and of today's prospects and problems regarding the restoration, maintenance and running of surviving examples. All in all, I hope that present *and* prospective owners will know where the car of their choice fits into MG's complex and interesting history.

No one would now deny that every T-Series MG had a great deal of character, and a liberal dash of that indefinable 'Abingdon touch'. You would expect that, of course, but if you understood the commercial and financial pressures on MG in this period you might be amazed that it could be so. Not to put too fine a point on it, once MG had been transferred from Lord Nuffield's personal possession to the Nuffield Group of companies in 1935, it was in the hands of the philistines. Nuffield was taken over (overtaken?) by B.M.C. in 1952, after which things got even worse. It was a miracle that the 'Abingdon touch' survived at all.

Each and every one of the four distinct T-Series types — TA, TB/TC, TD and TF — was designed under serious constraints, and in a hurry. At no time in the 20 years covered by the production of these cars was there an ordered, detailed and thoughtful development programme. The TA was designed, developed and prepared for sale in almost exactly a year, the TB in less and the TC in a matter of months after the end of World War Two. The TD progressed from an 'instant lash-up' taking two weeks' work to the production lines in well under a year, and the actual work involved in shaping the TF took less than a month. At no time during these processes did the designers and management employed by MG know what they might be expected to do in the next phase. For much of the time, indeed, neither Nuffield nor B.M.C. knew what the next phase might be.

In terms of numbers sold, and the time during which they were on the market, the least popular of the T-Series cars were the first and last models — the TA and the TF. Now, however, the TA is respected because of its rarity value, and for its links with the earlier generations of MG, while the TF is in great demand as the last of the traditional MGs. Yet Cecil Kimber and H. N. Charles would not have developed the TA if they had had more choice in the events of 1935, and John Thornley and Syd Enever had already shaped the MGA before being told to go back and reshape the TD into the TF!

One thing which emerges from this factual study, perhaps for the first time, is that there was a great deal more change between model and model than has been made clear before. The TB, for instance, was mechanically very different from the TA, with an entirely different engine, while the chassis and suspension of the TD was changed completely from that of the TC. The detailing of gearbox changes alone proves that no one in Nuffield seemed to have any idea about logical forward planning, about continuity, or about the way to ease spares, service and maintenance problems; three types of general internal arrangements, several sets of ratios, two different varieties of remote-control linkage, and many other minor changes tell it all.

In the last 10 years there has been a dramatic upsurge in the demand for, and reputation of, the T-Series MGs. In the years after the TF was dropped (especially when the MGA was in production), the value of all T-Series cars plummeted, and many were scrapped after their wooden-framed bodies had rotted away. By the time enthusiasts realized that the MGB was never going to be changed, improved, or replaced, it was almost too late to get any dealer or factory service support for alternative MGs. Now, it is a complete waste of time approaching British Leyland for anything except sympathy in rebuilding or maintaining a T-Series MG; even the last of the 'consumable' mechanical items went out-of-stock at the Cowley spares warehouses years ago.

However, once the 'classic car' movement began to mushroom in the 1970s, the demand for a T-Series car became intense. I well remember refusing to pay £400 for a near-immaculate TC in 1970, being convinced that cheaper and better examples could be found in the next county. I was piqued that the owner had not bothered to replace a rather secondhand hood and sidescreens, and wondered if I might ever find supplies to complete the job. Yes, I know, I was stupid. But how many people are turning up their noses at a Midget today?

For people in the market for a T-Series car, of course, there is one big problem. The supply is limited. Between 1936 and 1955 total production was 52,646 cars, of which more than half were TDs. My guess would be that less than 20,000 cars still exist, and that many of these will be in the United States. North American enthusiasts who read this book will be heartened to know that nearly 32,000 TCs, TDs and TFs were sold in the United States when new, and that many more have found their way to that country since then. After 1945 only 6,306 T-Series cars were sold in Britain, plus perhaps 2,000 to 2,500 of the TA/TB cars in 1936–39. Many of the cars which survive have certainly been exported since then.

The Bad News is that MG, and British Leyland, are no longer interested in these interesting sports cars. The Good News is that a number of fine firms have sprung up to supply anything from a piston ring to a complete body shell, a head gasket to an Owner's Manual, a lubrication chart to a speedometer. Whether you live in Great Britain or in North America, in Australia or Western Europe, the only problems connected with keeping your T-Series on the road are time — and money.

The specialist clubs catering for MGs are among the largest and most enthusiastic in the world. They are symptomatic of the enormous respect for the marque and the joy which goes with owning an MG. In the years to come, when motoring will become less of a hobby and more of an expensive chore, the T-Series cars will continue to be popular.

January 1980   GRAHAM ROBSON

Acknowledgements

Producing this purely factual book about T-Series MGs has been made a lot easier by many people — those who helped me with facts, figures and pictures, and those whose original researches, exploits and enthusiasm have all helped to make the cars so well documented.

Firstly, I would like to express my gratitude to the Jaguar-Rover-Triumph division of British Leyland (to which the MG marque is now attached) for their patience and understanding of my problems at a time when critics from all sides were hurling abuse at them for their tentative plans in connection with Abingdon's future. Glen Hutchinson, David Boole and Barry Crook (whose chart of production statistics is a triumph of detail) made much of my work possible.

Roche Bentley, Gordon Cobban and Glyn Giusti, of the two most important MG clubs (the MG Car Club and the MG Owners' Club) helped me to get the details right.

Michael Bowler, Ray Hutton, Lionel Burrell, Warren Allport and Susan Jones, all from that journalist's mine of information — IPC Transport Press (*Autocar and Thoroughbred & Classic Cars*) — helped me to locate otherwise-unobtainable pictures and references.

My very special gratitude goes to the Austin-Morris photographic department at Cowley, who let me comb through their voluminous and magnificently arranged archives for pictures. All but a handful of the illustrations in these pages are from Austin-Morris, without which — quite literally — a book of this nature would not be feasible to produce. To John Cooper, and to John Harvey, therefore, I am in debt.

GRAHAM ROBSON

CHAPTER 1

Ancestors and parentage

M-Type to PB

To MG enthusiasts the TA Midget of 1936 was in many respects a rather bewildering motor car. While it was recognizably the same sort of machine as all the previous MG Midgets, it was mechanically completely different. Although there were virtually no components in the TA which had been fitted to the PB Midget which it replaced, even a general inspection of its layout showed that it could only have been an MG sports car, designed by the same engineers.

However, although the TA was influenced by two distinctly different lines of ancestry, there was no doubt that its general character, which included a liberal dose of that elusive feature, 'the Abingdon touch', shone through. While, mechanically, the TA relied on a completely different set of Nuffield Group components and assemblies, its sporting behaviour was quite clearly related to that of the Midgets which had been in production — at Edmund Road, Cowley, and at Abingdon — since the spring of 1929. To understand the form of, and the thinking behind, the TA, it is necessary to analyze what MG had been doing in earlier years.

The story of how Cecil Kimber, who was manager of the Morris Garages business in Oxford at the beginning of the 1920s, came to inspire the building of modified Morris 'bull-nose' cars, and eventually to call them MGs, has been told often enough. All MG enthusiasts know that from these modest beginnings MG sports cars were built in a succession of small factories (all of which they soon outgrew) before the firm was moved to its permanent home at Abingdon, in a factory which had once been an extension of the Pavlove leather works. It is also important to the story, and particularly to the reason for the

Cecil Kimber, the man who inspired the development of the MG sports car in the 1920s and 1930s. As manager of Morris Garages, in Oxford, Kimber masterminded the fitting of special bodies on to 'bullnose' Morris cars in 1923 and soon began to develop more specialized 'MG' models. If there was such a thing as a between-wars MG stylist it was Kimber, and all the cars seemed to follow the same family style. Kimber left MG after a row with Nuffield's Miles Thomas in 1941, and was tragically killed in a railway accident at London's King's Cross station in 1945.

The one car, and two people, who had much to do with the development of the MG marque in the 1920s and 1930s. The car was the Morris Minor of 1928, and the two men were William Morris (later Lord Nuffield) and Miles Thomas (later Lord Thomas of Remenham). Morris Garages, which owned MG, was Morris' personal property until 1935. Thomas, at first, was the publicity manager of Morris Motors at Cowley, but later became managing director of Wolseley at a time when more Wolseley parts were being fitted to MGs in the late-1930s. During the Second World War he became vice-chairman of the Nuffield Group, but left at the end of 1947 after a row with Lord Nuffield. The Morris Minor of 1928, of course, formed the mechanical basis of the M-Type Midget.

The rolling chassis of the original M-Type MG Midget was virtually the same as that of the Morris Minor, except for trivial items like the wheel hub caps and the exhaust manifold, both of which carried MG octagons. It was the only MG sports car which shared another Morris or Wolseley model's chassis frame: even the Morris Minor announced in 1928 had a 'double drop' frame like this.

The original M-Type Midget of 1928–29, which went into production at Edmund Road, Cowley, in 1929. The famous MG radiator was a Kimber innovation in 1928 for the 18/80 and Midget models. Even though this was a very stark and mechanically simple model, with fabric-covered bodywork and sparse instrumentation, it was very popular as it originally sold for £175. The last of 3,235 M-Types was built at Abingdon in mid-1932.

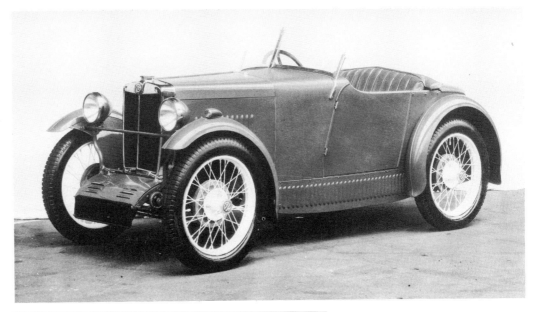

Getting into or out of the M-Type Midget's cockpit with the hood erect was not easy! The M-Type was a tiny car (with a wheelbase of 6ft 6 in) as this picture shows, and this particular example had the later steel-panelled body, but retained the familiar boat-style tail. So much of the general style to be carried on to the T-Series MGs was already apparent.

The assembly lines at Abingdon, soon after the move from Edmund Road had been completed in 1930. Fabric-bodied M-Type Midgets are being built on the far line, and the cars taking shape nearest the camera are Mark I 18/80 models. In neither case was a conveyor type of moving assembly line used, and apart from model changes this sort of scene was to be maintained for a good many years.

M-Type Midgets, all right-hand-drive, as every MG motor car was until the late-1940s, and Mark I 18/80 models, in the dispatch bay at Abingdon in 1930.

birth of the TA, to realize that William Morris, who was knighted at the beginning of 1929, personally owned Morris Garages (which controlled MG) as an entirely separate business from that of his large motor car manufacturing concern at Cowley.

At the end of 1929, therefore, when MG production (of M-Types and 18/80s) started up at Abingdon, the MG Car Company was a wholly-owned subsidiary of Morris Garages Ltd, which was William Morris' personal enterprise. So, too, was Wolseley Motors, of Birmingham, which Morris had taken over as a bankrupt concern at the end of 1926, after a rather sordid courtroom battle with Herbert Austin. Their principal assets were a great deal of under-used factory space, and some modern designs. On the other hand, the expanding Morris Motors group had already 'gone public' in 1926, though only to a limited degree as Morris himself retained all the Ordinary or 'voting' shares, and it included firms like SU Carburettors, Hollick & Pratt (body makers), the ex-Hotchkiss engine factories in Coventry, Osberton Radiators, and E. R. Wrigley (now turned into Morris Commercial); it was the largest car-making complex in Europe.

The business relationship, at that time, between the Morris Motors group, Wolseley and MG was rather relaxed. On William Morris' instructions, MG bought all their chassis components from one or other of the companies, but were allowed to fashion their own sports bodies, or have them made by outside suppliers. Bodies for the M-Type two-seater, therefore, were first built by Carbodies in Coventry, though the rest of the car was almost entirely based on the rolling chassis of the Morris Minor.

From the basis of the lovable, but not very fast, little M-Type Midget, therefore, Cecil Kimber began to fashion the ever more sporting MGs which were to follow in the 1930s. Although the M-Type remained in production, virtually unaltered, until mid-1932, its successors became progressively more special. Kimber and his chief designer, H. N. Charles (often without telling their proprietor *everything* they were planning) were always up to something.

Between 1929 and 1935, Kimber and Charles ran through dozens of 'EX' (for EXperimental) project numbers, and through most of the alphabet for the production cars which were marketed—there being Ms, Cs, Ds, Fs, Js, Ks, Ls, Qs, Ps, and

Rs, not necessarily in that order! During this period, in fact, two distinctly different strains of MG models were being evolved in the early and mid-1930s — all the Midgets having four-cylinder overhead-camshaft engines, and all the Magna/Magnette types having closely-related six-cylinder overhead-cam engines. Both types of engines started life as Wolseley designs, but as the years passed they were persistently and successfully modified for use exclusively by MG themselves.

It needs a truly dedicated MG historian to sort out all the sub-divisions of engines, chassis frames, types and model names produced in such a short time; however, in the case of all the Midgets which followed the M-Type, the same schematic layout of chassis frame was used, no matter how wheelbase or track dimensions might alter.

To follow the successful M-Type, Kimber wanted to be able to offer a car which was more obviously sporting, and special. The M-Type, after all, was little more than a rebodied version of the Morris Minor economy car, and used that model's chassis without modification, a chassis which featured 'dropped' side-member profiles alongside the clutch bell-housing, channel-section pressings, and a sharp kick-up over the back axle.

Kimber, like many distinguished managers before and since, looked around him at the opposition for inspiration, liked what he saw on the French market, and imported a 1.1-litre Rally two-seater for study. This car, among its many interesting features, had a simple underslung chassis (one which, in layout, had side members running in a straight line underneath the tubes of the back axle), which almost automatically encouraged the styling of low-slung and rakish-looking bodies.

Kimber and Charles therefore developed a brand-new underslung frame for use in EX120, the first of a whole series of special MG record cars, and it was from this general configuration that all MG Midgets of the 1930s and 1940s were to be derived. The first production MG to benefit from this new layout was the C-Type Montlhéry Midget of 1931, though the first *quantity* production MG to have an underslung frame was the F-Type Magna (with six-cylinder engine) announced in the autumn of 1931.

The heart of the MGs built between 1929 (the launch of the M-Type) and 1936 (when the PB was discontinued) was one or

An aerial shot of MG's factory at Abingdon, taken at the beginning of the 1930s soon after Morris Garages had taken it over from the Pavlova Leather Company. This shot is taken from the south, and the market town of Abingdon is on the right of the picture. Big extensions, into the undeveloped grassy area to the west of the factory (to the left, in this shot) were later built to look after expansion. British Leyland celebrated the Golden Anniversary (50 years) of the acquisition of this factory in 1979, then promptly announced that MG production on the site would cease in 1980.

Assembly of C-Type 'Montlhery' Midgets at Abingdon in 1931. Only 44 of these cars were built in the year during which they were on sale, and many were used for racing purposes. The C-Type was the first production MG to have the now-familiar underslung chassis-frame layout, which Cecil Kimber and H. N. Charles are reputed to have copied from the French Rally sports car of the period. This MG was the first to carry the characteristic twin humps on the scuttle, but had no doors, a cowled radiator and a Brooklands-type 'fishtail' silencer. The car in the background is an unsupercharged version, but has smooth racing-type tyres. The car in the foreground, by its tyre treads, seems to be intended for road use.

15

The M-Type's successor was the deliciously-styled little J2 Midget, announced in 1932. The J2 of 1932 retained fixed cycle-type front wings, which were replaced by these gracefully swept front wings from the autumn of 1933. Using a developed form of the C-Type and D-Type chassis frame, and improved 847cc engine, the J2 also brought together all the fine features so far pioneered on other MGs, including the twin-hump scuttle, cutaway doors, a fold-flat windscreen, slab-type fuel tank and spare wheel bolted to it. It is instructive to compare the swept-wing variety of J2 with the original TA which followed four years later.

The J2 chassis of 1932 showing how quickly the archetypal layout of 1930s MG Midget was maturing. This car, of course, used the 847cc engine, now in cross-flow-headed form.

16

A direct contrast with the J2's chassis design is that of this model, the PA Midget, announced in 1934 to replace the J-Type models. It was a different frame, with a longer wheelbase, but with much the same layout and many common components. The brakes — 12in diameter drums — were much larger and more powerful than those of the J2, although the three-bearing engine (which produced 35bhp from 847cc) was no more powerful than the J2's two-bearing type. The picture was taken at Abingdon, just before the rolling chassis was to be placed on the assembly line, immediately to the right of the picture.

The PB of 1935–36 in its final form was quite remarkably similar to the TA model which was shortly to replace it, as this illustration shows. It was also extremely similar to the J2 which had been made obsolete in 1934. PB models, made only for a few months, were effectively PAs with larger (939cc) and more powerful (43 bhp) engines.

Unlike the T-Types which followed, the P-Type Midgets could also be supplied with rather cramped four-seater bodies. This new car, exhibiting upholstery which was well-creased even before it was delivered, also shows the type of facia layout which Abingdon had evolved throughout the 1930s. On this car there is a combined rev-counter/speedometer ahead of the driver, while auxiliary instruments face the passenger. On this particular type of P-Type, the fuel tank was hidden by the rear body panel.

other of the single-overhead-camshaft engines which originated at Wolseley Motors in Birmingham. The four-cylinder unit, which went into production for the Morris Minor in 1928, had originally been designed by Wolseley for a stillborn 'Eight' of their own, before the takeover and rescue by Morris; the six-cylinder unit was developed directly from this, and was machined on the same tools.

They shared — at first — the distinctive feature of a vertical shaft drive from crankshaft to overhead camshaft at the front of the engine, which also doubled duty as the armature spindle for a vertical dynamo. It is worth noting that the original Magnas of 1931 had the same engine in all respects as that fitted to the despised Wolseley Hornet; to disguise these origins, therefore, Kimber instructed that sheet-metal 'disguise' should be added here and there to make the MG application look different!

In the first few years of the 1930s, the four-cylinder engines fitted to the Midgets and the six-cylinder engines fitted to Magnas and Magnettes became progressively more specialized. Although Wolseley continued to build the engines, those for MG eventually inherited completely different cylinder-heads, new camshafts, stronger crankshafts and many other details. Both types could be supercharged for competition purposes, or have their engine capacities altered to bring them within the limits of classes for certain types of racing. With the single exception of the engines fitted to PB Midgets in 1935–36, all shared the same cylinder-bore dimension of 57mm. In six years, standard-production engines with four cylinders had their power outputs increased from 20bhp at 4,000rpm to 43bhp at 5,500rpm (a power increase of 115 per cent), while those of the six-cylinder units went up more modestly, from 37bhp at 4,100rpm to 57bhp at 5,700rpm, which is a 54 per cent improvement.

The problem was not that the cars were getting no better (they most assuredly were improving), but that they sold progressively fewer and fewer in numbers. Even though Kimber encouraged an aggressive, active and demonstrably successful racing programme, which was supposed to be good for publicity and the marketing image, MG sales peaked at about 2,400 units a year in 1932, and fell steadily but persistently thereafter. At a time when the price of most things — food, clothing *and* cars — was tending to fall slightly (Happy Days!) that of an MG was rising. The M-Type of 1929–30 cost £175, whereas the PB of 1935 cost £222; the original F-Type Magna of 1931 was priced at £250, while the 1936 NA-Type Magnette cost £280. Not only this, but the competition, particularly from Singer, in the Midlands, was intensifying. It was not possible for MG to regain their position and increase sales by reducing prices, quite simply because MG was already a loss-making concern. With sales halved between 1932 and 1935, something had to be done.

By this time, too, big changes were nearing completion at Cowley, where Leonard Lord (that ruthless production-engineering expert who had joined Morris as part of the 'assets' of the Hotchkiss concern more than ten years earlier) had been given free rein to streamline the entire manufacturing process of the group. In 1935, too, Lord Nuffield (who had been ennobled in 1934) was persuaded to integrate his various business activities, and the result was the formation of the Nuffield Group.

It was as a prelude to this business upheaval that Cecil Kimber was told that the situation at Abingdon was unsatisfactory, that profits would have to be made in the future, and that the costly racing programme would have to be cancelled forthwith. He was also told that production of the Wolseley-based overhead-camshaft engines was soon to cease as part of the Lord-inspired rationalization programme, which meant that further building of PA/PB models and Magnettes would be impossible. Perhaps the biggest bombshell, however, came when he learned that both MG and Wolseley were to be transferred to Nuffield corporate ownership in July 1935, and that the autonomous MG design office was to be closed; all new MG design was to be centred on the Nuffield design offices at Cowley.

The withdrawal of MG from racing was announced in June 1935, and the amalgamation of Morris Motors, Wolseley and MG followed soon afterwards. Following the abrupt closure of the Abingdon design office, in which two important projects which were cancelled included a large-engined sports car, and

The fine lines of the PA/PB Midget, showing that even though there was a simple chassis with half-elliptic leaf front springs, it could be hidden neatly away from view. The MG octagon badge on the apron hid the hole giving access for the starting handle. 'JB', of course, was one of the local series of registrations used by the MG factory on their own cars.

improvements to the all-independent-suspension R-Type single-seater racing car, H. N. Charles was directed to work at Cowley.

Len Lord, then managing director of the Nuffield Group, who might charitably be described as having no soul-feeling at all for sports cars, and no real consideration for anyone else, initially said that he wanted to see an end to MG sports car production, and that he though Abingdon should prepare to build up a series of 'tarted-up' Morris and Wolseley models as MGs instead. It took little time, however, for him to be persuaded that this would be disastrous for MG's sporting image, if not outright commercial suicide. Although the plan for tarted-up Wolseleys went ahead (for, in truth, the SA/VA/WA models were little more than this), at very short notice he also told Charles, who was now under the general direction of Vic Oak (Nuffield's chief designer), to design a new sports car.

Charles, and Cecil Kimber (who influenced the design of the new model as much as possible, even though he was no longer the directing genius behind the project) did their very best within a very restrictive brief, and history shows us just how well they succeeded. For Kimber, in fact, it was a very welcome challenge, as in his day-to-day work at Abingdon he was now thoroughly dominated by the massive personality of Len Lord.

Since H. N. Charles had, at least, been allowed to develop a special chassis, the problem in creating the new car revolved around the choice and availability of an engine or engines, as it was no longer possible to consider using the fine overhead-camshaft engines which MG had developed so assiduously in the previous few years. Although new Wolseley models were being announced, even at that time, with the longer-stroke version of the overhead-camshaft engine, it was known by the designers that this was very much a final fling. In the spring of 1936, by which time the new MG sports car would have to be well on the way to readiness, new Wolseleys were due to be announced with overhead-valve versions of the well-known but hardly exciting Morris engine, which was made in Coventry. By the autumn, the last of those famous overhead-camshaft Wolseleys would be killed off.

Not only that, but Charles and Kimber had to face up to the fact that they were having to design just one new model to replace *both* existing ranges of MG sports cars — the PA/PB four-cylinder cars, and the N-Series six-cylinder Magnettes — which made their task doubly difficult. Their choice of engines, too, had to be confined to those already available, or due for imminent release, from the Nuffield engine-building empire at Coventry. This was not a very encouraging prospect, at first

The mechanical base from which important MG TA Midget components were developed was the Nuffield Series II design of rationalized 10hp and 12 hp family cars. Morris versions were announced in May 1935, and the Wolseleys followed rather later, in April 1936. This is the Morris 10 or 12 rolling chassis, launched with a side-valve engine and three-speed gearbox. All ports and manifolds are on the left side of the unit. When the Wolseleys appeared, only weeks before the launch of the TA Midget, they had an overhead-valve engine (with ports and manifolds on the right) and a four-speed gearbox.

If any Nuffield car could be said to have been the direct ancestor of the T-Series MGs it was this Wolseley 10/40 model of 1936, which had the overhead-valve 1,292cc engine and a four-speed manual gearbox with synchromesh on top and third gears. This studio picture of a Wolseley prototype is visually not quite correct as production cars had perforated disc ('easy clean') wheels and different bonnet-side decorations.

Three-quarter rear view of the 1936 Wolseley 10/40 model, complete with the correct bonnet panel decorations, the 'easy clean' wheels and the humped 'boot' (with no external access) to distinguish it from its cheaper relative, the Morris 10.

This meant that the engine for the new car would have to be developed — and developed very rapidly — from one of the '102mm' engines, the design which had first found a home in the 'bullnose' Morris in 1919, but which had since proliferated to such a degree that it was something of a statistician's nightmare. There were four-cylinder and six-cylinder types, ranging in size from 1,292cc to 2,561cc, but almost all of them were of a simple, very basic, side-valve configuration.

It came as something of a relief, therefore, for Charles to be told that an overhead-valve version of the 1,292cc engine — which was, indeed, a 'Ten' — was already scheduled for release in the new Wolseley 10/40 saloon in the spring of 1936, and that a tuned-up version of this engine could be made ready in time. The basic engines, incidentally, all had camshafts, valves and ports on the left side of the engine, which was perfectly normal for a side-valve unit. Overhead-valve derivatives kept their camshaft and the pushrods on the left, but had cylinder-head ports and manifolding on the right.

Right-side view of the engine/gearbox of the 1936 Wolseley 10/40 model (it could also be the 12/48, for there were no external differences), which formed the basis of the MG TA 1,292cc power train. These were the first '102mm' engines with ports and manifolds on the right.

Left-side view of the 10/40 Wolseley engine/gearbox, showing the cast-alloy sump pan, the distributor, dynamo and fan-drive arrangements.

glance, and since solving the conundrum was so vital to the new model's prospects, I must now examine the situation in some detail.

Henceforth, all Nuffield Group engines were to originate from Coventry, where the factory in Gosford Street was that taken over, complete with the current 'bullnose' engine design, from Hotchkiss & Cie in 1923. There were three basic engines — effectively the tiny one for the Morris Eight, the large one used in the biggest cars and in some light trucks, and the ubiquitous '102mm stroke' engine which had started it all way back in 1919.

In terms of the R.A.C. Rating of horsepower, the PA/PB Midget was a 'Nine', while the N-Series Magnette was a 'Twelve'. Charles and Kimber were told to look at one model which could span both markets, so it was reasonable that they should be planning to use an engine in the 'Ten' horsepower category. The little Morris Eight engine, therefore, was instantly discarded, as was the large-car design.

The engine choice, which might have been inevitable, also turned out to be very logical. All other MG models planned for introduction in the wake of the Morris-Wolseley-MG amalgamation and rationalization — the SA/WA touring cars with their six-cylinder engines, and the VA '1½-litre' model — which were mainly developed by Nuffield designers, all used derivatives of the same engine family. The result was that whereas in 1935 all MGs were based on the use of Wolseley-inspired overhead-camshaft engines, by the end of 1936 they would all be relying on one or other of the overhead-valve '102mm stroke' Morris units.

There was just time to finalize a higher engine tune, with twin SU carburettors and more efficient camshaft and manifolding. The Wolseley 10/40 engine developed a nominal 41bhp at 4,200rpm, while that fitted to the new Midget was rated at 50bhp at 4,500rpm (though various other figures have been quoted from a variety of sources).

To mate with this engine, however, there was absolutely no

The original 10/40 or 12/48 type of engine installed in a Wolseley chassis and body, showing how and why its carburettor layout was forced upon it by the restrictions of the engine bay.

Showing that ruthless rationalization of their products, though preached by Len Lord before he left Nuffield in 1936, had not been achieved, these two shots of the overhead-valve-engined Morris 10 engine/gearbox assembly (offered from autumn 1937), which was also shared with the Wolseley 10/40, reveal a different carburation layout, different manifolds, different cooling and fan location layouts and different dynamo position. This is why it is so difficult to recommend alternative sources for spare parts when restoring or maintaining rare T-Type MGs. Even the sump is a different casting, and includes a floating oil intake.

choice of gearboxes. The PB and Magnette boxes, with their combination of double-helical and straight-cut gears, but with no synchromesh, were due to die at the same time as the overhead-camshaft engines; to match up with the newly developed engine, now coded MPJG, the designers had to use the Nuffield gearbox normally married to the '102mm stroke' engine. This meant that they would have to use a cork-faced clutch plate, running in oil, backed by a four-speed gearbox without synchromesh, though this was no great disadvantage as no previous MG sports car had been fitted with synchromesh gears. However, Charles was allowed to develop a new remote-control gearchange, along with closer-ratio gears than those fitted to cars like the Wolseley 10/40. Things, indeed, could have been worse, for at the time design commenced the equivalent Morris Ten was still being fitted with a three-speed trans-

mission!

It was with such harrassing restrictions that the new type of Midget was speedily evolved in the second half of 1935. Although it was to carry a new title — the T-Series Midget (later, of course, retrospectively to be known as the TA) — and it was to be the hoped-for solution to many of MG's problems, it was not a car about which Kimber, Charles, or their staff at Abingdon could enthuse at first. It was likely to be fast enough, smart enough, and likely to give good value for money, but somehow there were doubts about its appeal. The loss of the overhead-camshaft engines, and most of all the loss of independence, had hurt them deeply. In every way, for sure, the layout and the philosophy of the TA was different from that of previous Midgets. Would the buying public take to it in sufficient numbers, or would the decline in Abingdon's fortunes continue?

CHAPTER 2

TA, TB and relatives

1936 to 1939

Once the design and production of an all-new Midget had been authorized in 1935, the efforts made to bring it into existence were immense. Given more time, no doubt, Charles might have laid out a different, more sophisticated, and arguably more attractive car. As it was, from the very beginning this was such a 'crash' programme that he could not afford to court possible problems by deviating from the well-proven Midget layout and lines. Even by the standards of the 1930s, when cars were very simply engineered, it was remarkable that the first car was delivered only a year after the first plans were laid. In view of Nuffield's reputation, at the time, for bumbling inefficiency, it was a miracle.

Several factors connected with the design were a great help. In particular, the chassis frame was extremely simple, the body shell was quick and easy to tool up, and the entire power train (except in detail) was both tooled and proven. Collectively these must have saved at least a year in the development process.

Although the T-Type Midget was only to be sold as a two-seater sports car (demand for the PA four-seater had been low), it was altogether more bulky and roomy than the superseded PB model. The new car was 8.5in longer overall, which allowed the passenger compartment to be more spacious, and the wheelbase was up to 7ft 10in, compared with the 7ft 3.3in of the PB. However, although the T-Type shared the same basic chassis dimensions of a 7ft 10in wheelbase and 3ft 9in tracks with the Q-Type racing Midget, it used an entirely new frame of a very familiar Abingdon pattern. The main side members were essentially straight and flat in both views, apart from a kicked-up section to clear the movement of the front axle, and cross-

The MG TA 1,292cc engine of 1936 in its original form, showing quite obvious similarities, and many common castings and components, to the Wolseley 10/40 engine. Manifolding and carburation, of course, are completely different, and the gearbox casing has a light-alloy extension holding the stubby gear-lever, which is out of shot. Note that on the TA, the carburettor air cleaner is on the rear of the cast-alloy manifold, tucked up against the bulkhead. In fact, the cleaner/carburettor layouts are noticeably different on each of the TA, TC, TD and TF series of Midgets, and (if original) give an immediate recognition point for enthusiasts.

Better than any blueprint is this illustration of the TA's rolling chassis, which was obligingly tipped on to its side for the benefit of the photographer. Thus revealed, the absolute simplicity of the chassis frame, with its slim but ruler-straight side-members and its rather rudimentary tubular cross-members, without any form of diagonal bracing, becomes obvious. Notice how the front lever-arm dampers work fore-and-aft, while the rear dampers are set across the frame. Front springs are mounted under the main chassis rails, while rear springs are well outboard of this line. Everything mechanical apart from the carburettor air-cleaner is neatly tucked inside the line of that frame. It cannot, however, have been at all stiff, either in bending or in torsion.

bracing was by four tubular sections. Like all recent Midgets, the frame was 'underslung' of the rear axle casing, but the new design's channel-section side members were boxed-in in the region of the front suspension and engine bay. By modern standards it looks incredibly flimsy, and probably was very flexible, as its resistance to torsional stresses must have been low. By 1930s standards, however, it was perfectly adequate for its job. The only sections, incidentally, needing any substantial tooling were those side members, and motor industry specialists tackled that sort of thing every day.

There was no time (and probably no cost allowance in the budget) for the new car to be given independent suspension such as the R-Type already had. Instead, the T-Type followed

PB practice with half-elliptic leaf springs at front and rear, along with cam-gear steering, and whereas the PB had used friction damping at the front and hydraulic lever-arm damping at the rear, the T-Series cars used Luvax hydraulic lever-arm dampers all round. Another feature was the new car's brakes, which were considerably *smaller* in diameter than those of the PB (9in in place of 12in), but were operated hydraulically by courtesy of Lockheed; all previous Midgets had used mechanical braking systems. As always, a fly-off type of handbrake was retained.

There could be no criticism from seasoned MG sports enthusiasts about the styling of the new car, which followed the same popular and rather rakish lines as those of the PBs and Magnettes which it replaced. As ever, the two-seater body shell

26

had an ash wooden framework, panelled in hand-worked or simply pressed steel panels. Assembly of the centre/rear section was at the Morris Bodies factory in Coventry, though complete and final assembly of all constituent items was carried out at Abingdon. Like the new breed of Magnettes and the SA model, both of which had been announced the previous autumn, this new type of Midget had a slatted type of radiator instead of the honeycomb favoured by earlier models. On the first cars, at least, there was a 15-gallon fuel tank, wire-spoke wheels with outside lacing, and P-Type rear wings.

However, although the type and even the detail of the chassis was familiar to MG enthusiasts, they had to come to terms with a completely different power train. From radiator cooling fan to drive-shafts it was all new, not new to Nuffield, of course, but unfamiliar to the sports-car buyers. They might, indeed, have noticed the launch of the Series II Morris 10s and 12s in 1935, and possibly the announcement of the 10/40 and 12/48 Wolseleys in April 1936, and the sharper-eyed would no doubt see the great mechanical similarities.

Indeed, it went much further than this. The engine, of the '102mm stroke' family, was related to that of the SA's 2,288cc production engine, and was seen to be very similar to that of the 1½-litre VA when this car was announced a few months later. The gearbox casing, indeed, was shared with all these aforementioned cars, though the MG's ratios were the closest yet developed. There was no synchromesh on the new T-Type model, as indeed there was not on the first production examples of the SA (but then, no MG yet sold had ever had a synchromesh change, though a Wilson preselector change had featured on K-Type Magnettes and other more specialized models). Also new to the T-Type Midget was the banjo-type spiral-bevel axle, with its 4.875:1 ratio, though once again this was one of the rationalized Nuffield components to be found on many other contemporary models.

To introduce such a new model, mechanically quite different if not more advanced, was a big gamble, at a time when MG's fortunes were in something approaching eclipse, and everyone waited with bated breath to see how the customers would react. In respect, however, they had nothing to fear, and though larger, heavier and faster than the superseded PB, and rated as a 'Ten' instead of a 'Nine', the T-Type was sold at exactly the same price of £222, and in those halcyon days there was no purchase

By comparison with the overhead shot, this side view of the TA's chassis shows that the main chassis members were not straight in side elevation. Straight under the rear axle, they kick up considerably to pass over the top of the front axle beam. The position of the steering wheel and the gear-lever (on its extension) shows just how far back in the chassis the driver and passenger are located.

Detail of the rear suspension, back axle and brakes of the original TA, which show, among other features, the trunnion location at the rear of the half-elliptic leaf spring, the way the frame is under-slung of the axle casing, and the Lockheed hydraulic brakes which, at 9in diameter, were considerably smaller than those superseded on the PB. The TA was the first-ever MG Midget to have hydraulic brakes, although a similar system had been announced for the SA saloons and tourers which were revealed in the autumn of 1935. Note the hydraulic lever-arm dampers behind the axle casing. The support bracket ahead of the casing is for one of the two six-volt batteries.

tax to boost the showroom price.

The Autocar and *The Motor* both took the same line in their technical analyses of the new car, published in late-June 1936. One magazine's headline was 'The Midget Grows Up', while the other merely placarded 'A Larger MG Midget'. *The Motor*, perhaps, went right over the top by sub-heading this with the comment that here was a new model 'Designed expressly for sports enthusiasts and competition work', which was a bit ambitious as MG were a bit breathless after producing the car, and certainly had not had much time to finalize the list of extras.

In those days the magazines would not have dreamed of suggesting that this was a cheapened model, compared with the PB, and even the road tests were not likely to say anything startling. *The Autocar*, however, summed up many testers' feel-ings by commenting that 'the new car achieves a more "solid" and impressive appearance', and that 'on the road the "feel" of the new car has undergone a change; the new Midget is softer, quieter and more flexible at low speeds'.

All this, of course, was intended to educate the reader that a real change had taken place in Charles' (and MG's) attitude to spring and damper settings, and to the creature comforts demanded by the customer. Not only did the 1936 buyer require room to drive without hunching himself up (there was 3in more width across the cockpit and 4in more height under an erect hood, compared with the PB), but he didn't neccessarily need a rasping exhaust note, and certainly didn't insist on bone-hard suspension. These factors, and the ability to put up a reasonably fast cross-country average without a constant fusillade of gear-

The first of the TA Midgets in the Cowley styling studio, showing a remarkable resemblance in its general layout and lines to the last of the PB Midgets, which it replaced from mid-1936. It was a noticeably larger car than any previous Midget, though its wheelbase of 7ft 10in was by no means the largest MG sports car yet. With the first of the overhead-valves lever to power a Midget, with more space, and with a rather softer and more relaxed ride, it took on a completely new character and attracted some criticism at first.

changes, made the T-Type Midget altogether easier to drive than its ancestors.

At this stage I must summarize the way in which the cars were built. Abingdon was merely an assembly factory, the only parts actually manufactured there being minor trim and furnishing items. The assembly line, at the time, was nothing more complicated than a raised 'runway', where the offside wheels were retained in a channel and the nearside wheels ran along unchannelled brickwork. Naturally enough, assembly started with the bare chassis frame, which was delivered, ready finished, from a specialist concern in the Midlands, and to which the front and rear axles and suspensions were speedily added to make a true rolling chassis out of the embryo car.

Engines machined and assembled at Morris Engines, Coventry, and gearboxes (also machined and built in the Midlands),

met each other at Abingdon and were fitted to the rolling chassis, after which the centre body (comprising bulkhead, floor, doors and tail sections already assembled at Morris Bodies, Coventry) was added. Radiators and sweeping front wings followed, then, after a mountain of extra work connecting hydraulics, electrics, trim and furnishings, the complete car was driven off the line, ready for an individual road test in the lanes of Oxfordshire. No Midget, of course, was built for stock, each car having been ordered by the dealer or distributor, either for a particular customer, or for his own small stocks.

Nuffield, at this time, were still in a state of some confusion following the forced merger of Wolseley and MG with Morris, the rapid rationalization of engines, body/chassis designs and administration, and the vast expansion of output at Morris Engines in Coventry. For MG, in fact, the T-Type Midget

In side view the TA Midget was longer and — if possible — even slightly sleeker than the PB Midget which it replaced. Trials enthusiasts noted with pleasure that all the compromises needed to produce a new model had not resulted in a poor ground clearance though that cast sump was clearly to need some shielding. With the hood erect, side visibility was adequate just so long as the celluloid side-screens were kept clean and free from scratches.

The TA Midget's neat facia, complete with wood facing, where the rev counter was placed squarely ahead of the driver and the speedometer was ahead of the passenger, with an enterprising driver and a nervous passenger, this must have produced all manner of problems. The gear-lever 'gate' is no longer visible, unlike on earlier Midgets, and the fly-off handbrake is situated on the passenger's side of the tunnel. There was a roll-type throttle pedal, and the clutch and brake pedals pivoted on an axis under the floor.

arrived at a really traumatic time, for not only was the PB Midget being phased-out, but the first SA saloons were being built and delivered, and there were preparations afoot to accept two other new models — the VA 1½-litre tourer and saloon — in the coming autumn.

Other historians have already pointed out the chaos which must have prevailed for a time. Although Abingdon had moved mountains to get the T-Type into production, they must have been dismayed to be told that changes were already inevitable. After 183 cars had been made — no more than two months' production of the new model — a more modern gearbox mechanism, in the same casing, was added, in which the ratios were slightly closer and synchromesh was provided on top and third gears; this happened at the same time as synchromesh was fitted to the SAs, but there seemed to be no reason for the original delay as the same type of synchromesh gearboxes had been fitted to Series II Morris models from May 1935 and to the related Wolseleys from April 1936!

During the life of the TA model, as it would become known when its successor was announced, there were few other significant mechanical changes. The rating of the 1,292cc engine was never made very clear at the time — a power output was never quoted when the model was announced, for instance — and several different ratings have since been quoted, ranging from 45bhp at 4,800rpm (which sounds low, particularly in view of the single-carburettor Wolseley 10/40's 41bhp rating) to

Various MG models taking shape on the assembly lines at Abingdon in the 1937–38 period. TAs are being built on the line furthest from the camera, while those on the other line are 1½-litre VA models, as is the car in the foreground. Parked in the background are SA 2-litre saloons.

Another view of the Abingdon assembly lines in 1936, with a line of new TA Midgets running in parallel with SA 2-litre saloons. In this view, the mounting for the TA's spare-wheel plinth is particularly obvious.

52.4bhp at 5,000rpm (which sounds suspiciously precise). At no time did the authoritative *Autocar Buyers' Guide* carry the rating in its tables, although suitable figures were supplied for the equivalent Morris and Wolseley models. The MPJG engine, however, was certainly improved during the period it was in production, and the figure most often quoted for the majority of engines was 50bhp at 4,500rpm, which accords well with the TA's road performance and maximum speed.

Body changes, too, were minimal. After the first 1,519 TAs had been built, in fact starting from Chassis Number TA1769 towards the end of 1937, the rear wings were widened and given a centre rib, and at the same time the fuel tank was narrowed slightly to make way for this change, the capacity being reduced to 13.5 gallons. At this time centre-lace wire wheels were adopted in place of the originals, still incidentally retaining that 2.5in wheel-rim width which sounds so ludicrously narrow to us now.

However, when the 1939 MG range was announced in August 1938, an additional body style was described for the TA — not a four-seater machine, but a smart and very attractive two-seater drophead coupe by Tickford. Although it was a factory-approved style, it was to be built at the Tickford works at Newport Pagnell (which is now occupied by Aston Martin), from partly completed TA models supplied from Abingdon.

Basically, the entire 'passenger box' — windscreen and pillars, doors, rear quarter and folding hood — were new, though the radiator, sweeping front wings, running boards, rear wings and fuel tank were standard TA items. (The prototype even had a sweeping tail which covered in the fuel tank, but this was never offered on production cars.) Doors had no cutaway sills, but their tops ran through from front to rear at bonnet-top height, and included wind-down door glasses and a window channel butting on to the windscreen. The screen itself was more substantial, had painted instead of chromed side rails, and could not be folded down. The fold-away hood did not disappear completely, nor could it be dismantled, which meant that the Tickford was not such a smart car when the hood was

furled. It could, however, be used partly erect, with the top rolled back behind the passengers' heads, as an alternative to being completely raised. In this latter position, with the glass windows wound up tight, it was a snug, if cramped, little coupe. Chromed hood irons on the rear quarters completed the picture.

Perhaps the two most important features, neither of which gained much attention at the time, were that the Tickford-bodied car was substantially wider across the seats (44in from door to door, compared with 40.5in for the Abingdon-built sports tourer), and that the windscreen wipers were pivoted from the base of the screen instead of from its rail and consequently the dangerously protruding wiper motor was hidden away. Both features would find a home in T-Series MGs of the future.

Very few of the TA Tickford models were built, which is hardly surprising, considering the short time the TA model was to remain in production after announcement of this body, and

Introduced in August 1938 for the TA, but later carried on for the TB models, was this very smart drophead coupe body by Tickford at Newport Pagnell. Although the front wings, running boards, radiator and bonnet panels were not changed, the scuttle panel, screen, doors and folding hood were entirely special. Semaphore indicators, wind-down door glasses and painted (as opposed to brightwork) screen pillars were all featured. The chassis was unaltered. Note that the hood could be folded back, but not dismantled completely.

It was possible to run the TA/TB Tickford model with its hood erect, but with the top (over the occupants' heads) furled back and tied neatly into a roll.

The Tickford-bodied TA/TB car at its smartest, with the hood completely erect and the supports locked in place. In this guise it was a very smart and snug little car. The tail treatment, featuring an enclosed fuel tank, was provided for this one prototype, but not used on production cars, which retained the exposed slab tank.

no doubt because of the increased price, which was £269 10s (£269.50). Although this was only £47.50 more than that of the standard car, in modern terms this equates to something like £600 in 1980 currency and was a considerable deterrent.

I must also mention that, as a private venture, there was an Airline coupe version of the TA, with styling rather like that of the N-Type and P-Type Airlines, in which different doors, sliding sidescreens and a sweeping fixed-head steel roof were grafted on to the basically standard body. These cars, marketed by H. W. Allingham, of London, were sold through the major MG dealers in London, University Motors, who were the con-cessionaires. However, the price, at £295, was even higher than that of the Tickford model which followed, and it is probable that only one or two were actually built.

At this stage I should review the TA's relationship with other MG models announced between 1935 and 1939. There were three of these — the SA, VA and WA, usually known as the 'SVW' series — and all were generally acknowledged to have been conceived by Nuffield rather than by MG, and to be fairly closely related to Wolseleys of the period. The TA had little in common with the SA/WA cars, which used much larger chassis, bodies and six-cylinder engines, though it is worth pointing out

The TB engine, which was fitted between spring and autumn 1939, fitted neatly into the engine bay originally designed to accommodate the rather bulkier TA unit. The SU petrol pump is mounted on the scuttle assembly, and the steering column runs very close to the starter motor.

The TA Midget gave way to the TB, in the spring of 1939, without the buying public being informed (presumably, they found out for themselves the first time they opened the bonnet!); the change from TA to TB was purely due to the adoption of the new XPAG 1,250cc engine, linked to a dry clutch, synchromesh on top, third *and* second gears, and a changed axle ratio to take account of the higher-revving engine. As can be seen from these two illustrations, the engine was not merely an adaptation of the old design, but was completely new in all respects. The

that the engines were derivatives of the ubiquitous '102mm stroke' Morris design, and that both gearbox and rear-axle casings were of the same structural layout.

The VA—the MG '1½-litre' announced in the autumn of 1936 —was a Nuffield design, but was much more closely related. Its engine was a 1,548cc overhead-valve unit, essentially the same as the TA's engine except that it had a 69.5mm cylinder bore in a different block and carburation differences, and it used the same gearbox except for different ratios. The rear axle was also structurally similar, except that it had a different ratio and a wider track. The chassis, suspensions, steering and bodywork were all entirely special.

However, the Nuffield Group were not content to leave things alone. Not only were two new generations of small Morris/Wolseley family cars being evolved (the Morris 10 Series M and the 8 Series E were both launched at the 1938 Earls Court Motor Show), but a brand new intermediate-size engine was being developed at Coventry, at the same time as a big new production factory was being built at Courthouse Green, in the suburbs of the city. The famous '102mm stroke' engine, was not only becoming long in the tooth, but was really too large to be produced as a small-capacity unit, such as was used in the Morris 10/Wolseley 10/MG TA cars. On the other hand, the side-valve engine used in the Morris Eight was unsuitable for obvious recognition points include the relocated air-cleaner (reclining across the engine rocker cover), the fatter and squatter oil filter body, the changed profile of the gearbox extension cover, and the more squat and compact shape of the engine block itself. Not immediately obvious is the fact that the new engine's block meets the sump face on the level of the crankshaft centre-line, while the MPJG unit of the TA had a block which wrapped round the crank bearings and met its sump face somewhat lower.

expansion, and nothing but a work-a-day prime mover. A new engine, to plug the gap, was therefore an obvious project to tackle.

Coded XPJM for Morris use, it was revealed in the autumn of 1938 as the power unit of the new Morris 10 Series M. The new unit, while conventional in every way, and with pushrod-operated overhead valves, was much more compact than the old '102mm stroke' engine, as it was based around a 90mm stroke and was not intended to be stretched with a great variety of different cylinder-bore dimensions. The cylinder block was squatter and altogether more robust, and the joint with the cast-alloy sump pan was at crankshaft centre-line level. Not only

this, but the new engine's cylinder-head had four exhaust ports instead of three (on the TA's engine the centre cylinders shared a siamesed exhaust port), and it was mated to a single-dry-plate clutch. In Morris 10 Series M guise, its dimensions were 63.5 × 90mm bore and stroke, giving a capacity of 1,140cc. Although the cylinder bore was the same as that of the TA's old-type engine, the cylinder centres and every other detail of the cylinder block were different; it was a new design in all respects. Even for the Morris 10 Series M it was mated to yet another version of the familiar Nuffield gearbox, in which there was synchromesh on top, third *and* second gears.

When the Wolseley 10 version of this car was announced in

Although there were no obvious visual changes when changing from the TA to the TB model, nor any badges to identify the cars, this illustration shows the very restricted vision available through the slots in the hood when it was erect. The bonnet side panels had different sets of cooling louvres, and the bulge below the near-side headlamp was to give clearance to the large dynamo of the XPAG engine. Ribbed rear wings were introduced during the run of the TA.

The 'in joke' for Nuffield behind this picture, taken in the Cowley styling studios, is that the numberplate is a fake. It denotes an MG T-Type, for which the retail price is £222! This, in fact, is the prototype MG TB Midget, of which only 379 production examples were built, which makes them something of a collector's rarity these days.

'Allo, allo, allo . . .' what's this? In fact, it is a mock-up of a proposed police car version of the TA/TB Midget, complete with radio aerial under the left-side running board and a siren mounted above the wing.

February 1939 (interestingly enough, with a separate chassis, whereas the Morris 10 Series M had unit-construction and many of the same body panels), Nuffield-watchers began to sense that something might be about to happen to the Midget. So it was, but interestingly MG did not announce the changes to the Midget until the autumn of 1939, months after they had been made!

During 1938 and the first months of 1939, a new and more highly tuned version of the new engine had been developed. This unit, coded XPAG, featured an enlarged cylinder bore of 66.5mm, which resulted in a capacity of 1,250cc and for British buyers this larger bore meant that the R.A.C. Rating would be increased to make the new car an 'Eleven'. New camshaft profiles, manifolding and twin SU carburettors — all very similar to those employed on the TA's engine — combined to give the XPAG engine a most encouraging power output of 54bhp at 5,200rpm.

At the end of April 1939, therefore, the last of 3,003 TA Midgets was built, and was immediately replaced on the assembly line at Abingdon by a new version of the car, called the TB. In chassis and bodywork terms, the car was absolutely unchanged; the engine and transmission, however, were completely different. The 1,250cc XPAG engine, with its single-dry-plate clutch, was mated to a revised gearbox (still in the same familiar casing) with yet another set of ratios and synchromesh on second gear. Because the new engine revved so much higher than the obsolete 1,292cc unit, the rear axle ratio was changed from 4.875:1 to 5.12:1, which made the new car slightly, but almost unnoticeably, more 'fussy' to drive. Not that any enthusiast complained, as the revised combination was smoother, livelier and more responsive.

A casual glance under the bonnet revealed not much difference in the appearance of the two engines, but an immediate recognition point was the disposition of the air-cleaner. This had been horizontally positioned on the TA, at the rear of the cast-alloy trunking, whereas on the TB it was mounted transversely, from a revised cast-alloy set of piping, and rested on the rocker cover. As far as the public was concerned, the only change announced in May was a marginal increase in price — to £225 for the two-seater tourer, and to £270 for the Tickford-bodied coupe.

There were, of course, hidden benefits which boded well for the future of the model, and indeed for the future of the MG marque itself, including details like the use of shell bearings for big-ends (they had been included as metalled connecting-rods for the TA), the dry-plate clutch, which was much more solid

An important near-relative of the TA/TB Midgets, produced at Abingdon from the middle of 1937 until the end of 1939, was the VA model, which was much more 'Nuffield' and much less 'Abingdon' than the Midgets, even though it was assembled at Abingdon. Although the chassis frame was unique, it used a larger-bore version of the TA's engine, with 1,548cc, and had the same basic gearbox and back axle, though with different ratios. Like the much larger SA/WA models, the VA (or 1½-litre as it was originally known) had a chassis frame with side-members swept up and over the back axle, and featured extra longitudinal members running back alongside the gearbox.

Chassis detail of the VA 1½-litre MG model, showing important differences, but also the use of some common components. The chassis side-members were boxed in a simple manner — something not yet adopted for a Midget. The wheelbase, of course, at 9ft 0in, was considerably longer than that of the Midgets.

The MG VA, in tourer form, as styled by Nuffield with additional touches by Cecil Kimber, showed an obvious family resemblance to the TA Midget with which it was a contemporary, although there was a 9ft 0in wheelbase and four full-size seats. Even so, there were virtually no common components in the two types of body. The three-quarter-rear view of the VA 1½-litre tourer emphasizes its significantly larger passenger compartment, and shows a definite family likeness to the four-seater touring shells produced for the P-series Midgets.

and suitable than before, and the fully counter-balanced crankshaft (which made tuning-up less of a risky business). The basic car, however, which had won the hearts of MG enthusiasts since its launch in 1936, was not changed, and seemed to be as popular as ever.

Herr Hitler, and his crazy and grandiose schemes for world domination and the 'Thousand Year Reich', intervened in September and brought all MG private car production speedily to a close. MG's 1940-model programme, in fact, was revealed immediately *after* war had been declared, which meant that no

sooner did the public at large know about the TB than they were denied the opportunity to buy one. In four months, only 379 TBs were made.

MG, however, moved off into their war effort, secure in the knowledge that their T-Series MGs, after a most unhappy birth, had already had a successful career. In no more than 38 months, 3,382 TAs and TBs had been built; if the rate was not as high as that achieved by the PA/PB models of 1934–36, the total sales were already higher, and indeed this was already the highest-selling series of MGs yet built.

One MG model which was not as popular as might have been expected — mainly because it looked a lot faster than it was — was the four-door saloon version of the MG VA 1½-litre, with coachwork by Morris Bodies. Its styling was very similar to the much larger SA/WA models, though its wheelbase was considerably shorter and there was less passenger space. As with other saloon cars of the period (including contemporary Morris and Wolseley models) there was enclosed luggage accommodation behind the seats; Morris and Wolseley cars of this size had no exterior access to the 'boot', while the VA had a let-down lid. A VA had marginally more power than the smaller TA engine, but was considerably heavier.

CHAPTER 3

TC — the postwar sensation

1945 to 1949

During the six years of World War Two the entire workforce of MG, at Abingdon and at Cowley, were kept far too busy to think very seriously about the cars they thought MG should begin making after the war was over. Unlike other firms in the British motor industry, the Nuffield Group did not go in for wholesale 'cheating' by getting on with private-car design when it should have been concentrating on building tanks, engines or aeroplanes.

Not only this, but in 1941 MG's loyal workforce had suffered a severe shock when Cecil Kimber abruptly left the firm, following a sudden and bitter row with Miles Thomas, who by then had become vice-chairman and managing director of the entire Nuffield Group (and therefore was Kimber's boss). The flareup was quite unconnected with MG's private-car business or its prospects, but with Kimber's way of obtaining war contracts without reference to his superiors at Cowley. Kimber then moved to Charlesworth, the Coventry-based ex-coachbuilding concern, to reorganize their facilities for improved war-time production, and a year later he moved on to Specialloid Pistons, in North London, to do the same job for them. But in February 1945, when he was still only 56 years old, Kimber was killed in a low-speed railway accident in the tunnels outside London's King's Cross Station.

However, although MG had lost their founder and enthusiastic guiding genius, they had not lost their collective love for sports cars. Following Kimber's dismissal, a new managing director, H. A. Ryder (ex-Morris Radiators) had been appointed, and had instantly struck up a rapport with the staff at MG who had been so shocked by recent events. It was Ryder, in

1945, who sparked off a speedy return to sports-car production, and who in fact realized that the only quick way to achieve this was by assembling new examples of the existing prewar design.

But even in conditions of extreme austerity, and with motorists all over the world screaming for new cars, MG still took time out to consider the improvements they would like to make to the TB to make it even more attractive to postwar buyers. The changes took six months to complete — almost as long as it took to design, tool *and* get the original M-Type into the showrooms — and they left the new car, the TC, looking almost exactly like the TB from which it was developed. In its general layout, its styling, performance and handling, the TC was very familiar indeed, and because British 'Pool' petrol was so much less effective than before, TCs were slightly slower than the 1939 TBs had been.

The most important change — and the most extensive, for significant changes were needed to the admittedly rudimentary body tooling at Morris Bodies in Coventry — was that the body was widened by nearly 4in across the seats without changing the basic chassis, wings, running-boards, or facia layout. This brought the shoulder-to-shoulder total width up to 44in, which was exactly the same figure as that offered by the TA/TB Tickford models. At the same time the seats were increased in size.

Other bodywork modifications included the provision of a battery box under the bonnet, housing a single 12-volt battery, in place of the twin six-volt batteries which had been carried on trays on the chassis frame, ahead of the rear axle, and were only accessible by lifting access flaps behind the seats.

There were also changes to the suspension. Luvax-Girling

Chassis detail of the TC model, as produced from 1945 to 1949, showing that the only significant difference compared with the 1939 TB was that the trunnion location of the rear springs had been abandoned in favour of a conventional shackel, and that the twin six-volt batteries had been moved from cradles ahead of the axle, and replaced by a single 12-volt battery on the bulkhead, behind the engine.

TC front suspension detail was like that of the TA and TB models, with short, stiff half-elliptic leaf springs under the chassis frame, and hydraulic lever-arm dampers mounted ahead of the axle, on the side of the main chassis members.

hydraulic lever-arm dampers were adopted in place of the original type, and at front and rear the traditional MG-type of sliding trunnion at the rear of the leaf spring was abandoned in favour of a conventional shackle arrangement. To keep the geometry virtually unchanged, the fixed pivot of the shackle was *below* the line of what had originally been the trunnion support. On the other hand, the same 4.50-19in tyres were retained on those incredibly spindly 2.5in rims. In modern terms the TC, while endowed with really sporting handling, had very little of that rather different quality, ultimate roadholding.

Although MG were preparing to face the motoring world with a model substantially the same as that made in 1939, the world itself was a very different place. In Britain, price levels had changed dramatically (it was now necessary to charge £375 for the TC, and for H.M. Government to extract nearly £105 extra in the new-fangled and hated purchase tax), and so had the economic climate. The nation's financial resources had been so comprehensively drained by the war effort that every industry

44

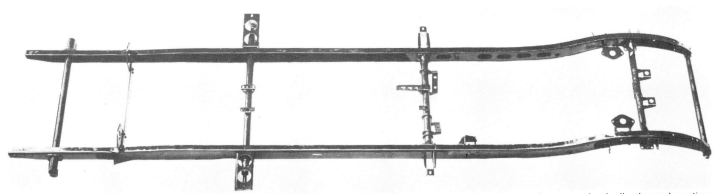

Yes, the TC chassis frame (a direct descendant of the TA/TB frame) really was as simple as that. The side-members were basically channel-section, though there was some boxing around the engine bay and transmission areas. No wonder it had been possible to tool-up for this new design in less than 12 months in 1935–36!

In this view of a complete TC Midget rolling chassis it is just possible to spot the rear spring shackles near the tail, and the relocation of the battery to a box on the bulkhead, above and behind the engine, is obvious. Not so clear here, even though the bulkhead-toeboard is in place, is that the width of the body on a TC was four inches greater than on TA/TB models.

Assembly of a TC begins, with this chassis and suspensions just beginning their journey down Abingdon's simple assembly line towards completion. The propeller shaft is not yet in place, and the engine/gearbox assembly is about to be craned into position.

'Dressing up' a TC Midget's bulkhead begins at Abingdon, with electrical and fuel lines going into place, along with battery fixings, the grommet for the steering column and many other details. It was in this state that the bulkhead joined the chassis frame, after the engine and transmission had been added. Note that, in this 1946–47 picture, the workman is busy on a right-hand-drive installation — no left-hand-drive TCs had yet been built.

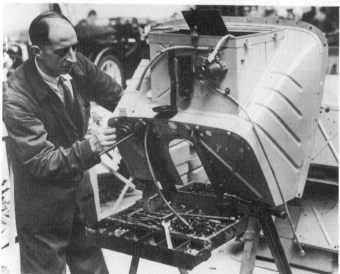

was being urged to export the major proportion of its output, so that much-needed hard currency (particularly American dollars) could be earned.

There was also a well-publicized shortage of sheet steel for the building of cars. In fact, there was not an acute steel shortage, but much of the available material was being directed into the rebuilding of housing and industrial plant which had been damaged by bombing in the previous few years, so the effect on the motor industry was just the same.

The authorities let it be known the sheet-steel allocations would be based on a company's export performance, so for Nuffield, who had exported a growing proportion of their cars in the late-1930s, the problem was at least familiar. However, for MG, who had relied to a great extent on their home sales, it was an entirely new experience. In the past, almost every export MG had gone to a territory we might then have called 'The Empire', whose people still drove resolutely on the left-hand side of the road, where British right-hand-steering cars were ideal, and where speedometers marked in miles-per-hour were

For the TB/TC model, introduced in 1939, Nuffield introduced a new XPAG engine, based on this brand-new standard design from Morris Engines at Coventry. Intended for the Morris and Wolseley 10s, the engine shown here was coded XPJM, and had a bore, stroke and capacity of 63.5 × 90mm, 1,140cc. Note the stylized 'M' for Morris on the trunking from the air-cleaner above the engine to the single SU carburettor.

understood. Now, for the first time ever, MG would have to consider making left-hand-drive sports cars.

Although it was a gloomy and depressing time to be in business in Britain, due to a combination of economic distress, food rationing, left-wing politics and fuel shortages, it was also a promising period for firms which were expanding. MG had come through the war without bomb damage at Abingdon (though the Morris Engines factories in Coventry were severely hit on more than one occasion), and as for Chancellor of the Exchequer Sir Stafford Cripps' exhortations to follow a one-model policy, they had already taken this decision in 1945.

They also found themselves in the happy position of receiving

a seemingly endless flow of orders for new TCs, even though the design was frankly obsolescent, and despite the fact that the number to be allocated to the home market was strictly limited; the problem was they could only hope to fulfil a fraction of these orders. First they had to complete modifications to the design, then order and secure delivery of new components, and then reassemble the facilities and the skilled workmen at Abingdon to build the cars. Many shop-floor workers had joined the forces during the war and some, alas, were killed in action. It was no wonder that MG struggled to get *any* TCs built before the end of 1945, and it was a miracle that 81 cars were built by then.

In 1946, however, the company's fighting spirit was

The Morris 10 Series M engine of 1938–39, coded XPJM, which is very obviously related to the larger-capacity XPAG unit which powered all Midgets built from March 1939 until 1955. On the Morris and Wolseley applications, a direct-action gear-change was used, though a remote-control mechanism was used on the Midget and VA 1½-litre models. In those days there was no legislation regarding the venting of crankcase fumes to the atmosphere, which was the purpose of the large-diameter tube angled back alongside the clutch housing.

unquenched, the supply problem began to ease, and no fewer than 1,675 TC Midgets left the assembly lines. Not only was this a record — no other Midget, or family of sports cars, had ever been built at such a rate in the 1930s (the PA, at about 1,100 cars a year in 1935, was the previous record-holder) — but 638 of them were exported, along with 36 CKD (Completely Knocked Down) kits of parts. It is only fair to point out that this was achieved without having to worry about the production of parallel lines of MG saloons (though this pleasurable piece of aggravation would reappear in 1947), and that the TC was now so familiar a model (its ancestors had been in production since 1936, after all) that in industry terms it virtually 'built itself'.

Even so, the record figures achieved were most encouraging.

At the time, of course, exports to the United States — at least *official* exports through a distributor network — had not yet begun, and it is important that this aspect of the TC's record should be put straight. Some years ago the TC became affectionately known as the British sports car which flooded North American markets in the 1940s, and as the car which paved the way for the greater success achieved by later MGs, Triumph TRs and Spitfires and Austin-Healeys. In fact, as MG's official records confirm, no TCs were sent to North America until the end of 1947 (and only six cars left Abingdon for the USA that year), and only 20 per cent of total TC production was delivered

Engine installation of a TC Midget (a TB would not have its battery in a box under the bulkhead) showing the very snug fit, while allowing adequate if not easy access to most items the keen owner needs to change, check or adjust from time to time. The bracing tubes from the radiator to the bulkhead should not be removed permanently, though of course they can be detached for access to the engine.

to the United States. It was the next model, the TD, which really set North American sports-car buffs by the ears, and the MGA which completed the domination.

No doubt the magic of driving and owning an MG sports car was introduced to the Americans during those terrifying, exhilarating and at times immensely satisfying days of World War Two. In almost every book, film or play the same *clichés* appeared — dashing Army or Air Force officer meets and falls for girl, dates her and rushes her out to dinners, dances and pubs in his noisy little British sports car. That sports car was invariably an MG Midget of one sort or another, and as in fiction, so it seemed to be in real life. In spite of stringent fuel rationing and

difficulties in obtaining spares and service, the troops — particularly the young officers — always managed to keep motoring, and they liked to do so in sports cars. The Americans, when they went home to a hoped-for prosperous future, took with them memories of war-time motoring and hoped to repeat such pleasures. For firms like MG it established a demand that they would take years to satisfy.

Once MG had gauged the demand for their TCs in North America, however, they quickly developed a proper 'USA' version of the design, though still without left-hand steering (not as easy a conversion as it sounds, as a change-over of pedals has to be carefully thought out), but with twin

A nice touch by the MG development engineers in the TC was that the bracing bar between radiator and bulkhead on the right side of the car was bent so that carburettors and manifolds had reasonable clearance, and could be removed if necessary without disturbing this tube.

TSMG—4**

Opposite page: A very smart new TC ready for delivery to its lucky owner in 1946 or 1947. From this viewpoint it is not easy to see that the entire centre-section of the body has been widened by four inches in the region of the seats, though the shape of front and rear wings, bonnet, and runningboards has not been changed.

The TC's slightly wider rear bodywork can just be picked out by the profile of the junction between the wings and the surround of the passenger compartment. No doubt the authorities would be horrified, these days, if a new model was proposed with such a large and potentially vulnerable fuel tank so close to the effects of a rear-end collision.

'Windtone' horns and twin tail-lamps. Tail and front side-lamps also included flashing direction indicators — at a time when other Midgets were not provided with any form of indicating equipment. The first official USA export model was built on Chassis Number 7380 in December 1948. Yet, in a way, it was all a waste of time, for the TC had only another year to live, and fewer of these specially modified TCs were to be delivered to North America than the number of original-specification cars which had already been delivered.

By the summer of 1949 the MG designers, now led by Syd Enever (for H. N. Charles had moved to Austin towards the end of the war), were working on a replacement for the TC, and no significant mechanical or styling changes were ever carried out to the model towards the end of its four-year life. Indeed, between 1945 and 1949 the specification changed remarkably little. For British buyers (if they could get their hands on a TC) the basic price of £375 on announcement in October 1945 rose to £412 10s (£412.50) in mid-1946, but it stayed at that price for the rest of the car's life, a remarkable achievement compared with price movements in the 1970s and early-1980s.

Although all the details are published in Appendix C, it is worth summarizing the markets in which TCs were delivered, as this gives a guide to where the surviving cars may be located. Only 2,001 of the 10,000 TCs built were originally sold in the

The TC's facia was not changed in general layout compared with the TA/TB models and kept the positions of the speedometer and the rev-counter widely separated. This, in fact, caused criticism, and would be altered when the TC model was replaced by the TD for 1950.

Assembly of TC Midgets going ahead full-blast in the late-1940s, with the first batch of YA saloons being built alongside them. Although all the TCs in this picture appear to have right-hand-drive layouts, they are also labelled as 'Nuffield Exports' and many are no doubt destined for North America.

One useful accessory sold for TA/TB/TC Midgets was this chromium-plated luggage rack which, although it partly obscured the spare wheel, still allowed the wheel to be extracted if needed. Filling the fuel tank, however, needed some care and dexterity, as the filler cap is hidden under the rails of the rack.

United States, mostly in 1948 and 1949. In spite of all the so-called rationing of sheet steel so that priority could be given to exports, no fewer than 3,403 TCs were delivered in Britain (34 per cent of total production), about 2,000 of them in the years 1946 and 1947 before the main export drive had matured. However, 4,591 cars were sent to other export markets — to many far-flung countries, but mainly to British Empire territories like Australia and South Africa. It is likely that in the 1950s and 1960s, when a TC was wrongly looked down upon as something only to be owned if the newer model could not be located, many TCs found their way to other countries. The problem, as outlined later in the book, was that the wooden-

framed bodies, which, frankly, were built down to a price, tended to deteriorate rapidly in some climates. One wonders if more than a quarter of all TCs ever built have survived?

In performance and roadholding terms, a TC was very much on a par with the TB from which it evolved and with the TD which replaced it, which is to say that it could almost reach an 80mph maximum speed when in good trim, accelerate to 60mph from rest in perhaps 23 seconds, and return fuel consumption figures of better than 30mpg. Even at the time the TC was in production this was no more than average sporting performance for a car of this price, but by modern standards it begins to look rather slow; any self-respecting small family car except the Mini

Visually no different from the pre-war TB, the post-war TC was received with acclaim in the 'austerity' years. Over a period of time, however, the transparent side-screens and quarter 'windows' behind the doors tend to become scratched and go partly opaque. Replacements, however, are still readily available.

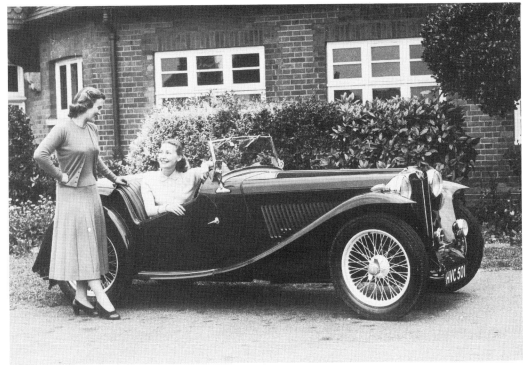

The implication of this TC publicity shot, posed with models, was not only that you attracted pretty girls by owning such a sports car, but that they could drive around with you in the same smart clothes. The truth about TC motoring, however, was rather less sybaritic.

I am not sure how to treat this picture, for it shows a team of 'traffic cops' from Warwickshire collecting six new TC sports cars, presumably to be able to catch, apprehend and subsequently prosecute the fast drivers of other sports cars. Somehow I don't think their peaked hats would stay on for long if they were driving the TCs with the hoods down.

should be able to out-sprint it, and certainly use a lot less fuel.

The TC's attraction, however, centred around its character — that elusive substance which you cannot always define, and certainly not buy in cans or freezer-packs in supermarkets. It had the sort of handling, roadholding and response which made any driving task a pleasure; a journey in a TC, even in cold and dismal weather, could be turned into a pleasure by the manner in which it was completed.

Ultimate roadholding, of course, was not that brilliant (nor could it be, due to the skinny tyres), but the handling was nicely balanced and, in modern parlance, the TC was very 'chuckable'. The steering, of course, was very direct, with only 1.5 turns

from lock to lock. This, together with the close-to-chest driving position and the instant and thoroughbred reaction of the chassis to steering movement, meant that it was a pleasure to hustle a TC along a winding road. The suspension, however, was very firm indeed (factory records show that the front springs had a mean rate of 270lb/in and the rears were rated at 228lb/in), though not nearly as hard as that of the TA and TB models, the front springs of which were so hard that the ride was joggly on all but the smoothest main road or motorway surfaces.

However, it was asking too much of customers to keep on taking delivery of cars whose design was rooted in the mid-1930s, and whose philosophy had been founded by Cecil

Kimber at the end of the 1920s. There was a good deal of charm built into a TC, but there were no bumpers, no heater, not enough space and no modern styling. Even though demand held up well as 1949 opened, it was thought time to begin designing a replacement for the TC. For the first time in 13 years, a change of style was due from Abingdon.

A sad day for traditionalists, in November 1949, when the last of the TC Midgets is pushed off the assembly line at Abingdon. All in all, 10,000 TCs were built in just over four years, and the model was replaced by the TD, which had an altogether different pedigree. The car on the line behind the TC is a YA saloon, with which the new car had much in common.

Mudplugging and racing

TA and TC — including Cream Crackers and Musketeers

MG's sudden and unexpected withdrawal from motor racing, in mid-1935, came as a shock to the company's customers, and even to many members of the staff. Although Cecil Kimber had to accept the Nuffield-inspired decision, and even put out a carefully-worded statement supporting it, he most certainly did not agree with it. It seems certain that he was behind any encouragement that could be given to MG owners in the way of technical advice, or clandestine development and preparation, to use their cars in one form of motor sport or another.

But from the middle of 1935 there could be no official MG involvement in motor racing, and even the record-breaking attempts headed by 'Goldie' Gardner were only approved by Lord Nuffield after a great deal of persuasion on Kimber's part. The EX135 record car, however, which achieved such phenomenal straight-line speeds in 1938 and 1939, bore absolutely no relation to current T-Series production cars as it used much-developed overhead-camshaft Magnette engines and chassis.

Neither the TA, which had an unsuitable engine, nor the TB, which was only available for a very short time, figured in significant Brooklands, Donington or Southport racing results between 1936 and 1939. In the field of sporting trials, however, it was an entirely different story, and it is here that a few very special TAs achieved something approaching glory for themselves.

The British 'sporting trial' was a form of motor sport not found anywhere else in the world. A descendant of the original British trials and rallies of Edwardian times, and coming to great popularity in the 1920s and early-1930s, the basic premise of a trial was that the organizers found muddy, rocky and steep tracks, usually on private ground, and challenged competitors to urge their highly-modified cars to the top of the 'Observed Sections'. High performance was not necessary, but good traction was, for the winner was not the one who achieved the highest speeds, but whose car managed to keep going up all (or most) of the sections. As a sport it was cheap, cheerful and almost entirely classless.

However, although trials of the 1920s were often won by saloons, by the 1930s the events had become so specialized that to be a winner one needed a rather singularly-developed lightweight sports car. Car preparation and the professionalism of competitors advanced more or less in step with the guile of the organizers. Cars gained special 'knobbly' tyres, locked axles, wide-ratio gearboxes and more powerful engines at the same time as surplus weight was cast away and lightweight materials were adopted. To match this, organizers found more and more really awful sections with which to tax the drivers, and after a time a real element of danger began to join the proceedings. Real bravery was needed to tackle horrifying declivities where there was a constant danger of the car rolling over — to one side, or to turn over backwards — especially if, as often happened, all traction was lost and the car had to be slid rather helplessly down to the start of the climb again. The truly classic, if somewhat easier events, were the Exeter, Land's End and Edinburgh Trials — all three of which survive to this day. The more concentrated events like the Colmore and Gloucester Trials needed more skill, but attracted fewer entries.

In the 1930s it was against this background that a whole series of 'one-make' teams evolved, using cars as diverse as Austin

Two of the famous 'Cream Cracker' TA Midgets, the works-sponsored trials team which in 1938 were originally equipped with 1,548cc (VA-size) versions of the ubiquitous Morris Motors engine, a size which was increased to no less than 1,708cc later in the year. BBL 78 was habitually driven by Maurice Toulmin, and other team members included Ken Crawford and Johnny Jones. As is obvious, the cars had cut-down bodies with cycle-type wings, light-alloy body panels, jacked-up front springs and pressed-steel sump pans. The knobbly tyres — banned from the end of 1938 — gave quite phenomenal traction.

One of the famous 'Cream Cracker' TAs, theoretically 'owned' by their drivers, but in reality a works-sponsored team, financed and organized by Abingdon. The light blade-type mudguards are obvious, as is the general layout of the cut-down bodywork, but this shot must have been requested in a hurry, for the car has knobbly front tyres and standard-treaded rears, with two knobbly spares!

The XPAG engine, although never designed to be a competition engine, proved to be surprisingly robust and tunable. This shows one of the more radically 'Stage' tuned engines which could be supplied from Abingdon for TC/TD/TF models, complete with a belt-driven Marshall supercharger.

Sevens and Allards, Singer Nines — and MGs. Without ignoring altogether the glamorous Tailwaggers, Grasshoppers and Candidi Provocatores featuring other marques, it is a fact that *the* most famous teams of all were based on MGs — the Cream Crackers, the Three Musketeers and, to a lesser extent, the Highlanders. The Crackers and the Musketeers, as each team was usually known, were eventually nothing less than works-supported ventures.

In fact the first of these MG teams to be formed — the Cream Crackers, in 1934 — was a private venture. Three drivers later to become well-known as works exponents — Maurice Toulmin, J. A. Macdermid and Jack Bastock — bought PA-type Midgets,

painted them in Abingdon's 'standard' livery of chocolate-and-cream, and began to gain success all over the country.

By 1935 a more obviously works-sponsored team of NE Magnettes had appeared — also painted chocolate-and-cream, but named the Three Musketeers, with each car appropriately carrying a name — Athos, Porthos and Aramis, after the characters in the original Alexandre Dumas novel. By the end of that year, however, MG had become more circumspect in their support of trials cars, had sold off the Magnettes, and the two teams were realigned. The Musketeer Magnettes were driven in 1936 by Bastock, Macdermid and Archie Langley, while the Cracker team was supplied with new PB Midgets to be driven by Maurice Toulmin, Johnny Jones and Ken Crawford.

Another year of success was almost embarrassingly complete, and the sponsored teams looked forward to greater things in 1937. As the overhead-camshaft MGs were now out of production, Abingdon provided two completely new sets of modified TAs. In theory these were sold to the team drivers, but the Abingdon registration numbers fooled no one, and it soon became generally known that MG were making maintenance allowances, paying travel and on-event expenses, and had agreed to take the tired cars back at the end of the season.

There had been minor changes of livery — the Crackers retaining their chocolate-and-cream finish, while the Musketeers changed over to a bright red paint job. For the record, the Crackers team used cars registered ABL 960, ABL 962 and ABL 964, while the Musketeers used ABL 961, ABL 963 and ABL 965.

Compared with the last two sets of overhead-camshaft works trials cars, the six TAs were much closer to standard, though they looked distinctive enough. The 1,292cc engines (about which the tuning experts still knew very little) were virtually unmodified on these 1937 models, except for raised compression ratios, though Wolseley ratios were used in place of MG ratios in the gearbox; this gave a bottom-gear ratio of 19.45:1 instead of 16.47:1, which was a great advantage when faced with really steep hills like Juniper and Leckhampton in the Cotswolds. The MG type of cast-alloy sump was retained at first, but it was hardly surprising that one team car received a cracked sump when skidding across a rock on its very first event (the Exeter Trial of 1937), after which pressed-steel Wolseley-type

Two famous teams of 'sporting trials' drivers of the later-1930s were the 'Cream Crackers' and the 'Three Musketeers', which began operating in 1934 with privately-owned but Abingdon-prepared cars. PAs, Magnettes and PBs were eventually used, and what were effectively works cars soon came to dominate the 'mud-plugging' scene. For 1937, with the TA now in production in Abingdon, both teams were provided with new and much-modified TA trials specials. This is the 1937 'Cream Cracker' team (R to L: Maurice Toulmin, Ken Crawford and Johnny Jones) in ABL 960, ABL 962 and ABL 964. The 'Musketeers' used ABL 961, ABL 963 and ABL 965. To distinguish the two teams, these 'Crackers' retained the well-known Abingdon colours of chocolate and cream (which explains their title) whereas the 'Musketeers' cars were bright red. Among the many special fittings were Wolseley-type gearboxes with low first and second gears, tiny J2-type mudgards and light-alloy panels. *(The Autocar)*

sump pans were used instead. Surprisingly, sump guards were not used, which in view of the awful condition of many section surfaces, seems to have been a brave omission. The TA's Nuffield-type back axle, too, was much more robust than that used on the old overhead-cam types, and the days of a roadside repair seemed to be over.

In spite of the cars being rather heavier than previous team cars (even though they all used aluminium bonnets and other panels, along with cycle-type front wings, they carried two spare wheels which rather upset the other gains) they had a very successful year. The Crackers won the M.C.C.'s Team Championship that year (the M.C.C. was responsible for organizing the Exeter, Land's End and Edinburgh Trials), and towards the end of the year 'Colonel' Maurice Toulmin shared the Experts' Trial outright victory with Godfrey Imhof — also in a TA Midget. There were several victories in the team-award contests, while Langley won the Liverpool M.C.'s Jeans Gold Cup Trial outright, Macdermid won the 'Brighton-Beer' (which visited neither place as it happens!) and tied for best performance in the Gloucester Trial.

There were so many successes, major and minor, team and individual, that MG were happy to provide six new cars for the 1938 season. Two of the Cracker team cars were sent to Scotland for 1938, for use by the Highlanders.

The sextet of 1938 cars were very different from the 1937 examples, and a different philosophy was followed for each of the two English teams. The Crackers, still retaining their chocolate-and-cream livery, were treated to a new set of TAs with enlarged engines, while the Musketeers (red-painted as usual) had TAs with supercharged engines.

The three Cracker cars — registered BBL 78, BBL 79 and BBL 80 — started life at the beginning of 1938 with 1,548cc VA-type engines (69.5mm cylinder bore), allied to MG gearbox ratios, steeply cambered front springs (to increase the ground clearance over the vulnerable sump) and very hard damper settings. The same type of light-alloy bodies, with tiny fixed cycle-type wings, were retained. However, competition to these MG teams was now so intense that it was decided that more power and torque was needed. By mid-summer all three cars had been given bored-out engines, labelled as 1,708cc, which meant that they had 73mm-bore pistons, not a size used on any

Maurice Toulmin's 'Cream Cracker' TA — one of the second batch of heavily-modified (including 1.7-litre engine) cars built by Abingdon as their works trials cars for the 1938 season — in big trouble on Ditch Lane in the Mid-Surrey Automobile Club's Experts' Trial of November 1938. That hill is *steep* — look at the way the spectators are struggling to keep their feet. Toulmin won his class in this event, which was held in Somerset and Devon. Note for enthusiasts and collectors — the other cars in the 1938 series had registration numbers up to and including BBL 84. *(The Autocar)*

other four-cylinder version of this ubiquitous engine, but one which was about to be standardized on the 2.56-litre six-cylinder WA-type MG saloon and tourer. (Cecil Kimber did not resent spending money on special equipment, but this was a rationalization which could not be missed.)

The new Musketeers cars — registered BBL 82, BBL 83 and BBL 84 — were rather different. Although their chassis and lightweight body equipment was the same as that used by the Crackers (which must have been useful from time to time when one member wanted a spare part which he was not carrying), their engines were of standard displacement, but used a Marshall supercharger and produced something like 70–75bhp.

For the second successive year, the Crackers won the M.C.C.'s much-coveted Team Championship, while many individual and team trophies were won by one or other of the drivers and their team-mates. At the end of the year Maurice Toulmin won his class in the Mid-Surrey A.C.'s Experts' Trial, though he had to give best to an Austin Seven in the fight for outright victory.

The autumn of 1938 was a difficult time for the trials fraternity. Not only was there the Munich political crisis to worry about, and the re-armament programme and sales recession in private motoring which went with it, but there were serious changes in trials-car specifications to be conquered. Alarmed by

Johnny Jones' 'Cream Cracker' TA just getting round a dry but rough hairpin in one of the many sporting trials which these Abingdon-prepared machines entered between 1937 and 1939. Note the fat special knobbly trials tyres urging the TA up the steep hill. The charming lady passenger's expression tells us that she is convinced that the car is going to hit the bank a mighty blow. *(The Autocar)*

public complaint about trials, the congestion they caused and the mess they left behind on public roads, the R.A.C.'s motor sport administrators brought in a ban on special competition tyres for 1939. Unhappily for the two works teams, their TAs seem to have been affected more adversely than most of their competitors, and during the winter of 1938–39 they began to lose out consistently to the big Allards and the Grasshopper Austins. For the Crackers, the final blow came early in 1939 when Maurice Toulmin married and retired from the sport, whereupon the team was disbanded and never reformed. The Musketeers lost Macdermid to a project to build a rear-engined trials car, but his place in the TA was taken by Dickie Green. The 1938 Musketeers cars carried on in 1939, when the trials scene was well-and-truly in decline (just as the R.A.C. had intended that it should be), but they managed to win team prizes in the Land's End and Edinburgh Trials, while Green himself won the Barnstaple Trial.

This, however, was the end of MG's involvement with trials teams, as indeed it was for other manufacturers. After the end of World War Two it was a long time before there was enough petrol for long-distance trials to take place again, and by then rallies had become popular in their place. Although the Exeter and the Land's End Trials continue to attract large entries, the mass of more localized trials have disappeared.

Although the TB was in production for too short a time for it to be used in any form of works team, there were four years in which TC usage could be encouraged. MG, however, could only do this in a rather clandestine way, as they were still banned from motor racing by Lord Nuffield's edict, and for a time there were no trials or rallies due to the shortage of fuel for such frivolities. It was only by supporting their most successful private owners that they could keep up the interest at Abingdon, and among their customers.

It took time, of course, to discover that the XPAG engine, though based on a very work-a-day design, was remarkably tunable. Supercharging, of course, was the easy way to liberate more power, but for events where such things were banned tuning had to be carried out by conventional means. Before the end of the TC's life, however, two private owners — George Phillips and Dick Jacobs — had gained a modicum of factory support for their modified TC cars. Phillips, of course, was to become *Autosport*'s chief photographer when that now-famous magazine started up in 1950, while Dick Jacobs had been appointed an MG dealer, at Woodford, in 1946. While Jacobs used a standard-looking TC for a couple of seasons, and then progressed to an MG special in 1949, Phillips used a very special TC, which had an altogether unique lightweight and more rounded body, and carried the appropriate registration number of MG 7185.

It was Jacobs and Phillips, after much nagging away at MG boss John Thornley, who persuaded MG to enter a trio of standard TCs for the first Production Car Race to be held in Britain, at Silverstone in the B.R.D.C.'s meeting sponsored by

A. B. Langley's 1938 supercharged 'Musketeer' TA trickling through one of the fords at Kineton, in the Cotswolds, on his way to tackling the steep and rutted climb that lies above it. These TAs (the other team cars were BBL 82 and BBL 83) were painted red, and wore special competition tyres. In those days, headgear was somewhat more orthodox than it has now become. The front suspension was raised on jacked-up springs to improve the clearance of the sump pan over the boulders which abounded on such sections. *(The Autocar)*

the *Daily Express*. The three cars were to be driven by Jacobs, Phillips and Ted Lund, and were faced with hot opposition from the 1½-litre HRGs. After a very disappointing first practice day, Jacobs' car was modified with 17in wheels from his own special in place of the narrow 19in production-car wheels; this, along with fatter-section tyres, produced an impressive improvement in Silverstone lap speed. Unfortunately, there is no fairy-tale happy ending. For much of the race Jacobs was second in his class to Eric Thompson's HRG, but at one point he left the track and smote a straw bale rather hard. The result was that the running order was upset, and after one hour's racing the MGs finished well down the field as a whole, fourth, fifth and sixth behind the larger-engined HRGs after averaging nearly 69mph — still a great achievement bearing in mind the cars' maximum speed of not more than 75–80mph.

The Phillips MG TC special, although not a works car, had works assistance, and was subsequently a vital spark to the events which eventually led to the evolution of the MGA for 1955, and therefore it merits attention. Phillips had bought the TC for racing in Britain and elsewhere, but had decided that the aerodynamics of the standard body shell were not at all satisfactory for this purpose, and had evolved a special style with rounded contours and a much lower scuttle line, although he retained the cycle-type wings.

Prior to driving it in the Le Mans 24-Hours race in 1949, he entered it for the B.R.D.C.'s Isle of Man race meeting, with Dick Jacobs as his co-driver. However, the car was not ready for this event, and it had to be taken to Le Mans without a long-distance work-out. It started well, settled down comfortably, but came to a halt out on the circuit in the 19th hour due to electrical failure. Even then, it could have been restarted if the mechanic had been able to give rather less obvious assistance, but this was seen by officials, and the car was disqualified. Phillips and his co-driver 'Curly' Dryden were most upset.

A year later, in June 1950, the car started its second Le Mans race, this time with considerable support from MG, particularly in regard to the engine. On this occasion there was no mistake, and Phillips, with co-driver Eric Winterbottom, were rewarded with a finish, second in the 1½-litre class behind a works Jowett Jupiter, and 18th overall. It was this performance which led to the building of a very special car for Phillips to use in 1951.

Langley again, tackling the fearsome Leckhampton climb in the 1938 Colmore Trial in his supercharged 'Musketeer' TA, which was nicknamed 'Aramis'. The other 'Musketeers', naturally enough, were 'Athos' (MacDermid) and 'Porthos' (Bastock). The only way to beat such dreadful hills was with competition tyres, locked differentials, a great deal of power and much determination, which every member of the team had in full measure. *(The Autocar)*

CHAPTER 5

TD and TD II

1950 to 1953

In the two years during which the TC was at the height of its popularity — 1948 and 1949 — great changes were taking place in the Nuffield Group. Not only had Sir Miles Thomas left the firm, following a predictable row with Lord Nuffield, and wholesale management changes had taken place, but the first generation of new postwar models had begun to appear on the production lines at Cowley. All had an effect, in one way or another, on the shaping of a successor to the TC.

By 1949 Abingdon's production lines were humming with activity, and were by no means confined to the assembly of sports cars. In 1947 the first of the postwar MG saloons — the YA — had started to be made, and by the end of 1948 a convertible version (the YT) had joined it. During 1949 further rationalization of Nuffield's production facilities led to assembly of Riley RM-Series 1½-litre and 2½-litre models being transferred from Coventry to Abingdon. By the summer of that year, therefore, the TC was effectively out-numbered by non-sports cars; during the year 2,813 TCs were built, compared with 1,969 Y-Types and 2,166 Rileys.

Of equal commercial importance were the mechanical developments at Cowley. During 1948 the last of the 1930s-type Morris and Wolseley models was phased-out, to be replaced by new Morris Minors, Oxfords and related Wolseleys. There were serious implications for MG. They would now be the sole user of the overhead-valve XP-Type engine, of the long-established four-speed gearbox, and of the spiral-bevel back axle. Even though Lord Nuffield's ideas of rationalization were by no means as far-reaching and logical as those of Len Lord had been, they had to wonder how long this would be allowed to continue?

The complication, too, was that the Y-Type MG saloon and tourer shared some common basic components with the TC (engine and gearbox castings and many internal items), while the YA saloon's body shell used the same basic passenger cabin, pressings, glass and hardware as that of the four-door Morris Eight Series E, which had now become obsolete, having been replaced by the Morris Minor. Its chassis and independent front suspension, too, was unique, which must have made it a somewhat uneconomic proposition to build at the rate of no more than 2,000 units a year.

During 1949, however, it became clear that MG sports-car customers, particularly those from overseas, were beginning to ask for something more modern, perhaps rather more civilized, and certainly a little more sophisticated than the TA/TB/TC family of cars they had been offered for so long.

Years earlier, the so-called 'experts' at Cowley might have dreamed up their own project to succeed the TC (styling mock-ups were, indeed, built in 1948, bearing some resemblance in style and detail to the Morris Minor), but their collective ego had been bruised by the failure of the YT tourer, and earlier by the less-than-rapturous response given to the VA tourer and saloon models. Therefore, as had happened before, and would happen again, MG staff, led now by Jack Tatlow (a well-liked ex-Riley manager), were asked to put up proposals for a new model.

Within two weeks, without actually drawing a thing, but by the time-honoured method of building a prototype from the ground up, Syd Enever, Alec Hounslow and their tiny staff had produced a new car — by the simple expedient of chopping five

In 1948, when Nuffield were already beginning to think about a replacement for the very traditionally-styled TC Midget, they built this mock-up in the Cowley styling studio. It is a mercy that it was never put into production, for although it was indeed a thoroughly modern shape (for the day) it was by no means as distinctive as later ideas for a full-width MG sports car proved to be. Many Morris Minor components were used in this study, and the nose was obviously shaped by the same team.

Introduced in 1947, although a 1938–39 design, was the four-door 1¼-litre MG YA saloon. Its body shell was based on that of the Morris Eight Series E, which had been launched in the autumn of 1938, even before the TB sports car was phased into production, and its special chassis frame included independent suspension designed by Alec Issigonis. Intended as a 1940–41 model, its release was stifled by the Second World War.

An historic motor car — actually the first prototype to use the independent front suspension later adopted for the MG YA saloons and T tourers, later still by the TD and TF sports cars, and carried on today in modified form for the MGB sports cars. The date is 1939, and at Cowley the car was identified, actually badged, as a *Morris* 10. Alec Issigonis had designed the independent suspension for the Morris Eight Series E and Morris 10 Series M, but on cost grounds it was frozen out in favour of a beam-axle design. This prototype is even more important than one might think, for a study of the car's underside shows that the car was indeed a Morris 10 Series M, which had a unit-construction body shell, and that the entire suspension, steering and cross-member is grafted to that shell.

inches out of a YA-Type chassis frame and welding-up the remains, and by cobbling up a TC body to fit. It was not exactly the car they thought should be built, but it was the type of car which the ever-practical MG men thought made the best technical, commercial and product-planning sense. In this simple 'blacksmith' manner, the bare bones of the world-famous TD sports car came together.

The design philosophy was a little more involved. Enever had decided that a new sports car to replace the TC must have a more rigid chassis frame which would not distort so much under extreme bending and torsional stress, and that it should also have independent front suspension. TC experience had also suggested that a softer ride coupled with more wheel movement would be a definite sales feature — and of course the car would have to look more up-to-date than the TC.

The styling, in effect, could be left until last, since the new body shell would be built by traditional coachbuilding methods at the Morris Bodies Branch factory in Coventry. 'Cutting and shutting' a YA chassis frame — which offered almost everything needed, due to its box-section side members and its coil-spring independent front suspension — was a logical solution to the

problem for one 'demonstration' prototype, even if it was not the final answer.

It is time, now, to study the origins of the YA saloon and chassis, from which this work was generated. Back in 1937, when a new series of Nuffield cars was being developed, Alec Issigonis was in charge of suspension development at Cowley, and Gerald Palmer had recently arrived to take over the MG design section, such as it was, from H. N. Charles. The Series III Morris and Wolseley cars were announced late in 1937, and for 1938–39 work was concentrated on the Morris Ten Series M, which had the first-ever Nuffield pressed-steel monocoque body/chassis unit, and on the Morris Eight Series E, which retained a separate chassis frame. Alec Issigonis had wanted to endow the Ten with coil-spring independent front suspension, but was overruled on cost grounds, and Gerald Palmer remembers that one of his first jobs was to develop a beam axle to take its place. The Eight Series E, on the other hand, had beam-axle suspension as a matter of course.

These cars were announced before the 1938 Earls Court Motor Show. During 1939 the Wolseley Ten arrived, which was based on the Ten Series M except that it had a separate chassis, while the Wolseley Eight (based on the Series E) was literally killed-off at the last minute by the outbreak of World War Two. In the meantime, work was going ahead on a new MG saloon at Cowley — the Y-Type. This new model, which at first glance sounded so unpromising because it was something of an amalgam of Ten Series M, Eight Series E and special new parts, was due for launch as a 1941 model, but due to the war was put right back to 1947. Its pedigree is vital to the story of the TD.

In effect, the Y-Type saloon used the basis of a Morris Eight/Wolseley Eight four-door body shell, but it had a specially swept tail and rear wings, a new and rather more traditional nose including a vertical MG radiator, and a wheelbase of 8ft 3in, which was no less than 10in longer than that of the basic body. Whereas the Morris and Wolseley derivatives shared a beam front axle and a common chassis frame, the MG had a new long-wheelbase chassis frame, and the coil spring independent front suspension originally designed for the monocoque 'Ten'. The new front suspension also included the use of rack-and-pinion steering, which had never before been used on an MG or Nuffield model of any type. This steering layout was mechanically much more precise and efficient than the Bishop cam used on earlier T-Series models, and made accurate handling very much easier.

All very confusing, but the power train story was even more so. The 'base' car, the Eight Series E, used a side-valve 918cc engine and the smallest Morris four-speed gearbox, while the Wolseley was scheduled to have an overhead-valve version of that. The MG, however, was to be treated to a detuned MG TB type of 1,250cc engine, such as was fitted to the Morris and Wolseley Tens, and a modified version of the gearbox to be found on these cars. It also had a type of semi-remote-control gearchange not used on the MG or on the Morris, but found on the Wolseley Ten!

So far, so good, except to point out that the chassis frame of the MG Y-Type was underslung at the rear, in traditional MG fashion, whereas that fitted under the Morris and Wolseley versions of the same body shell was swept up and over the axle. This, incidentally, was one of Nuffield's standardized late-

This was the rolling chassis of the MG YA saloon of 1947, which was the true ancestor of the TD and TF sports cars. The box-section chassis was entirely new and had little resemblance to that of the Morris Eight Series E, from which car the body shell of the YA was substantially modified. It is worth noting, however, that whereas the Series E's frame had side-members swept up and over the front and rear axles, that of the YA was underslung of the rear axle. Other points to note are the gear-change, which was very different from that of the existing TC, and the disc wheels.

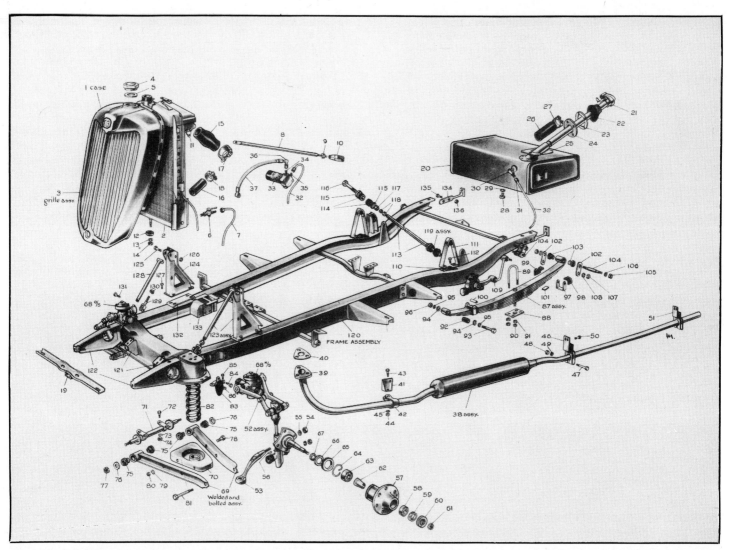

An 'exploded' drawing of the YA saloon chassis frame showing the double-channel type of box-section side-members, the independent front suspension and the much more robust sections compared with those of the TC sports car. At the rear, however, the side-members were underslung of the rear axle, which restricted rebound movement of the suspension.

1930s type of spiral-bevel units.

This brief survey of the Nuffield design philosophy which produced such a variety of models from only a limited number of 'building blocks' is needed to show how and why the MG Y-Type saloon came into being at all, and perhaps how it came to be retained in 1949 as a basis for the next sports car. Once the Abingdon-built 'lash-up' had been completed, merely to prove that such things were possible, it was shipped over to Cowley for the formal design work to proceed.

The TD then took shape rapidly, with several important differences from the hastily built Abingdon car. Although the Y-Type's coil-spring independent front suspension was retained (it still survives, in general layout, on the last of the MGBs being built in 1980), along with the general outline of the strong box-section Y-Type chassis frame, a new frame was designed, with its main side members swept up and over the line of the back axle, to allow for more rear-wheel movement (and provide a softer ride).

Mechanically, however, the TD's layout was familiar. The maximum output of the 1,250cc engine was exactly as it had been for the TC, though it was now distinguished with a circular oil-bath air-cleaner mounted atop the valve-gear cover. The basic features of the gearbox, too, were as found on the TC models, though yet again the gear ratios were slightly altered internally, and there was a new type of remote-control mechanism. On the TA/TB/TC box the light-alloy extension had sprouted directly from the top of the main casing; on the TD, the relatively new gearbox extension produced for the MG Y-Type/Wolseley Ten model was used, and a new light-alloy remote-control housing was bolted to it, with a mating face at an angle to the output shaft. The back axle, too, was new to MG, being a new rationalized Nuffield hypoid type (the first hypoid-bevel axle to be used on an MG) also found on the Morris Minor.

Apart from the demonstrably rigid chassis frame, the two other important features of the new car were that it was given rack-and-pinion steering (like that of the Y-Type) and that it was only offered with pressed-steel disc wheels. No previous MG Midget had ever been sold with disc wheels, so this change (made on cost-saving grounds by Nuffield) caused a real storm. Not only were disc wheels standard, but they were very ugly,

Assembly of MG YA saloons in progress at Abingdon, showing off the single-carburettor installation and the way the separate front wings are about to be bolted on to the pressed-steel body shell. The independent front suspension is obvious at this point, but will soon be obscured by the wings.

and wire-spoke wheels were not even offered as optional extras. Another feature, unnoticed because they were hidden away, were the two-leading-shoe front brakes, which were rather more powerful than the leading-and-trailing brakes used on the TC model. Another innovation of the chassis, also unnoticed because it could not be seen, was the hoop of tubular steel over the passengers' legs, which connected the main chassis members to the scuttle. This, in fact, was not incorporated until the first small batch of TDs had been built, by which time it was clear that an unacceptable degree of scuttle shake was present; the fitment of the tube alleviated the problem, and since it also gave some degree of accident roll-over protection, it also provided some favourable publicity.

Formed on the same wheelbase of 7ft 10in as the other

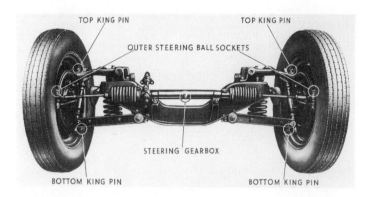

The famous MG TD/TF/MGA/MGB independent-front-suspension layout, which has only been modified in detail since it was designed in 1938 by Alec Issigonis. A feature is the dual purpose top wishbones, which are pivoted on the fulcrum of the lever-arm hydraulic dampers bolted to the top of the cross-member. In these mechanized modern times, many of us have forgotten just how much greasing and attention were needed by such installations — even on this simple set-up, there were no fewer than seven grease nipples, which really needed attention every 500 miles!

T-Series Midgets (there was still room for tradition at Abingdon!), the TD offered a much more squat and purposeful stance. The combination of considerably more compact wheels and tyres (a tyre section of 5.50-15in for the TD compared with 4.50-19in on the TC, with a wheel-rim width up to 4.0in from 2.5in), and the Y-Type's wider tracks — no less than 5in greater at the rear — did great things for both looks and general road behaviour. Even though the suspension was much softer than before, and roll was much more noticeable, the roadholding limit and passenger comfort were considerably improved.

The body style, however, was something of a disappointment. Although every panel was different from that of the TC and there was a new facia arrangement the result was still strictly traditional, for there were separate flowing front wings, running boards, separate head-lamps, a vertical MG radiator, centrally hinged bonnet, and an exposed fuel tank at the rear. Those MG features still thought to be important — including a wiper motor bolted to the screen rail, an exposed spare wheel fitted to a cradle behind the fuel tank and cutaway doors with simple stick-in weather protection — were all retained, as was the classic coach-built type of body construction featuring pressed and hand-formed steel panelling on a simply-tooled ash frame. There was still no provision for a fresh-air heater, or for a built-in radio, for separate adjustment of the seats, for direction indicators, or for anything other than the most basic protection against inclement weather. One thing, however, was quite new — the inclusion of sturdy chrome-plated bumpers at front and rear. This was not perhaps what the enthusiast might have wanted (and it certainly added to the weight), but it was becoming essential for the many MGs which were to be sold in North America, where the average driver of mass-produced 'Detroit iron' was not at all delicate or particular in his close-parking manoeuvres.

Although the TD's layout, its frame and its general construction was more substantial than that of the TC, it was also heavier. The unladen weight of the 1950 model TD was 1,930lb, which compared rather badly with the 1,735lb of a TC, representing an increase of 11 per cent.

Apart from its slightly changed air-cleaner layout, the XPAG engine in the TD was otherwise the same as that used in the TC, with the same peak power and torque figures — 54bhp at 5,200rpm, 64lb ft at 2,600rpm. Without the blessing of the smaller-diameter 15in tyres, therefore, the TD would definitely have been less lively than the obsolete TC. Independent road testers' figures, in fact, show that the TD *was* slightly slower than the TC, even though its gearing was the lowest of any T-Series production car.

Not that this seemed to deter the customer, and with the steel supply position in Britain easing rapidly, production and sales rose steeply. Whereas the TC's best year had been 1948, when 3,085 cars had been built (about 60 a week on average), in its first year no less than 4,767 TDs were built (about 95 to 100 cars a week allowing for holidays), and this figure was immediately surpassed by a new record of 7,451 cars in 1951, followed by 10,838 cars in 1952. In that year, more TDs were made in 12 months than the TC could notch up in more than four years of production.

The success was due to several factors. The supply problem (of raw materials) eased at the right time, the new design and styling (the use of independent front suspension and the first styling changes since 1936) were welcomed, and the North American love affair with British sports cars was blossoming well. Indeed, it was the mass exports achieved by MG which were the making of the boom in TD sales, as the statistics prove; only 1,646 TDs, compared with 3,408 TCs, were originally delivered to British customers.

The biggest single factor in the huge export success of the TD, not often noted by other observers, was connected with its price. Although the Nuffield Group had not been successful in keeping the cost of the new model down to that of the superseded TC, in export markets they benefited by one important factor — devaluation. In September 1949, just as production of TCs was beginning to draw to a close, the British government devalued the parity of the pound from $4.03 to $2.80, a move which immediately made their products cheaper and therefore more attractive, to overseas customers.

At home, a 1950 TD cost £445 (basic), compared with £412 10s (£412.50) for the TC. In North America, on the other hand, a 1950 TD sold for $1,850 f.o.b. New York, compared with no less than $2,395 for the last of the TCs. Without the devaluation, which could not have come at a better time for MG, the new car might have cost more than $2,600, which would certainly have killed its chances.

Yet, despite this success, the TD was a very controversial model, which gave rise to spirited correspondence in motoring magazines and to innumerable arguments at motor club meetings and any other place where two or more MG owners or enthusiasts might gather. The lack of real modernization in the

MG's half-way house between the YA saloon and a full-blooded sports car was the YT sports tourer, introduced in the autumn of 1948 and sold only in export markets. It differed from the YA saloon by having the higher engine tune of the TC Midget, but it was too heavy and cumbersome to have really sparkling performance. The body shell, incidentally, has absolutely nothing in common with that of the VA tourer of 1937–39, even though there is a family resemblance.

styling and of performance improvements were talking points, as was the fitment of the big bumpers, but most hated of all were the very unstylish disc wheels. Perhaps this would not have mattered as much if wire-spoke wheels had been available at extra cost.

One reason advanced for the disc-wheel decision was that the layout and geometry of the new-fangled independent front suspension made it very difficult for satisfactory wire-spoke wheels to be designed, but it is certain that a degree of cost-saving also entered into it. There was no question of interchangeability at first, of course, for the YA saloon and its closely-related YT tourer used 5.25-16in tyres on 16in wheels, whereas the TD was given 5.50-15in tyres on 15in wheels. TD and YA interchangeability had been an important factor during the design

process, but this was not one of the important items commonized; it would not be until the autumn of 1951, when the YA became the YB, that the saloon would have the same size wheels as the TD, and even then they would not be of the perforated type.

Improvements, however, clearly had to be made to maintain the impetus of the TD's original success. For this and other reasons connected with the rather unsettled technical climate in the Nuffield (later, B.M.C.) Group, the TD eventually came in for more detail development and change than any of the other T-Series cars. This is best summarized by a look at the point at which changes began to take place. Important engine and transmission changes were made at Engine Number 9408, and a whole series of minor improvements followed up to about too, on a Midget, the chassis side-members were not parallel, but splayed-out from front to rear. The frame was, in every way, stiffer and more substantial than that of the obsolete TC frame. If you compare it with that of the YA saloon, there are obvious similarities, but the TD has its side-members swept up and over the back axle. The roll cage over the passengers' legs was to support the scuttle, provide a modicum of protection against accidents, and cut down on scuttle shake.

Engine Number 25,000. Chassis changes began at about the same time, and ceased by the beginning of 1953, at which time the TF was rapidly being designed and prepared for production. In terms of cars' production dates, those built up to the Abingdon works holiday of summer 1951 were essentially to the original specification, while those built between August 1951 and the end of 1952 went through the process of detail change.

I will deal with chassis and bodywork changes first. There was speedy action to deal with complaints about the plain road wheels. Dick Jacobs and George Phillips had already tested a TD with a view to racing it by March 1950, and the first works car raced at the end of May 1950 (see Chapter 7). Even before that first car — FMO 885 — was raced, it was fitted with a set of perforated disc road wheels to improve the flow of cooling air

over the brakes, and these were immediately adopted for tuned cars. Such wheels began to be fitted to production-line models from the early-summer of 1950, originally for cars delivered to United States and Canadian customers, but by the end of 1950 they were standard equipment on every TD. Much later — in 1952, it seems — wire-spoke wheels were once again theoretically made available. I say this because few people seem to have discovered this, MG did not seem at all anxious to publicize the fact, and the author cannot recall ever seeing a new or nearly-new TD with wire wheels fitted; these were, however, the wheels which became a much more popular extra on the TF model of 1953–55. It follows that even today a TD owner would have little difficulty in fitting the TF wire-wheel equipment to his TD, as long as he ensured that he was using the hubs and

The TD's front suspension, as finalized for production, and little changed from the prototype layout of 1938–39. Even by 1950, other firms were beginning to consider using telescopic dampers, but MG remained faithful to lever-arm hydraulic dampers with internal pistons, and these are retained to this day on MGBs. The fact that this car carried perforated disc wheels labels the chassis as one built after about the first year of production.

The TD's rear frame and suspension layout shows many important advances compared with that of the TC. The frame itself has massive box-section side-members, which were much stiffer to resist bending and torsion. The frame was swept up and over the back axle, so that more bump-and-rebound movement could be provided. A new hypoid-bevel axle was fitted, not only with product rationalization in mind, but to slightly lower the line of the propeller shaft. Not obvious here, but immediately noted by potential customers, was that the wheels were not only smaller in diameter (15in instead of the TC's 19in) but they were also steel discs with stud-and-nut fixing arrangements. Until the TF was introduced in 1953 there would be no wire-wheel option on a two-seater MG sports car.

minor items necessary to complete the conversion.

In the late-autumn of 1952, for '1953 models', four changes were made at slightly different Chassis Number introduction points (I know this sounds illogical, but it was the way the newly-formed B.M.C. concern seemed to operate!). From Chassis Number TD21303 the original moulded type of stop/tail-lamps were discarded in favour of circular lamps, which were cheaper and arguably rather smarter; these were to be carried on for the TF. From Chassis Number TD22371 all cars sent to the North American continent were given flashing indicator equipment; this had been standardized on the North

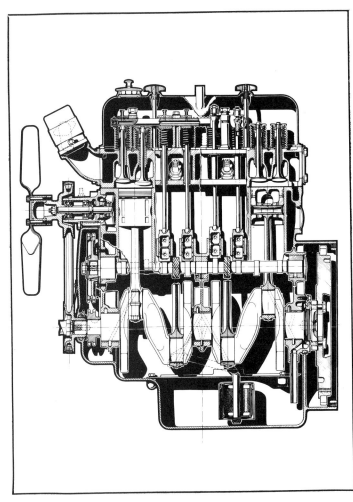

This longitudinal engineering section of the TD's 1,250cc engine shows the robust nature of the counterbalanced three-bearing crankshaft (that of the TA had no counterbalancing weights) and the simple but effective layout of the valve gear. Camshaft drive was by chain, from the nose of the crankshaft, and both oil pump and distributor drives were from skew gears on the camshaft. The water pump is in a recess in front of the block, driven by belt from the nose of the crank, and the same spindle also drives the cooling fan.

The near-side illustration of the TD engine shows that although there are several obvious visual differences compared with that fitted to the TC, the XPAG unit is substantially the same as that first specified in 1939. The oil filter bowl is now horizontal, and more closely linked with the oil pump, the sump is a different shape, and the engine mounting arrangements have also been altered.

American TCs, but then dropped for the original export-market TDs. TDs built for other territories, including Great Britain, had no indicators of any description. Crazy!

In the meantime, from TD22315, all cars had inherited a new windscreen-wiper layout. The motor was still exposed, and still fitted to the screen rail, but to give a marginal improvement in case of accidents it was now at the centre of the screen rail where it was less likely to come into contact with either occupant's head. Only cars built between about December 1952 and September 1953 were so equipped, and there was to be an even more fundamental change for the TF which followed. The final electrical change, introduced at about the same time (I regret that I have not traced the introduction point) was that the head-lamp dip-switch was located on the floor near the clutch pedal instead of on the facia panel.

The engine and transmission changes, though rarely obvious, were significant, and have since given rise to a great deal of confusion. There was, and is, a misunderstanding of two different types — those cars known as the TD II and the TD Mark 2; the use of the word 'Mark' is important. I ought to spend a little time explaining the differences. Basically, a TD II was the standard production car built from the late-summer of 1951 (meaning a 1952 or 1953 model-year car), with Engine Numbers prefixed with TD II . . . A Mark 2 was the name given to the more specialized and much rarer TDs intended for use in competition, which were fitted with one of the various MG 'Stage' tuning kits and incorporated chassis changes; this car is described more completely in Chapter 7. There were TD Mark 2s in existence from the early-summer of 1950, but the 1950 and 1951 Mark 2s carried TD . . . Engine Numbers.

This carburettor-side shot of an engine/gearbox assembly shows that it is intended for use in a TD Mark II. The carburation/air cleaner arrangement is, yet again, altered (compared with the TA and the TB/TC) and a cylindrical air-cleaner now sits on top of the rocker cover. The carburettors on TD Mark II models had 1½in chokes and larger bodies than the previous 1¼in components. Although the gearbox is substantially the same as that fitted to the TB/TC range, the gear-lever, extension and selector arrangements are completely different. The gearbox top casing now carries a plain cover, there is a new rear extension, which houses the rear of extended selector rods, and carries a new remote-control casting and the gear linkage. The rear extension was developed for the Wolseley 10 and YA MG saloon, but the remote control was especially designed for the TD.

Engine installation of the 1,250cc XPAG unit in the TD Midget. Though general arrangements, compared with the TC, are much the same, various accessories have been relocated, and the battery is now exposed in a tray, rather than hidden away in a box.

MG TD Midgets in production at Abingdon on the line which built TC's until the end of 1949. Because the TD was, in many ways, similar to the YA, it was possible for both to be assembled in sequence, as this shot proves, for the fifth car in line is a YA. By this time, Riley production was also centred at Abingdon, and the RM-type cars were assembled on an adjoining line.

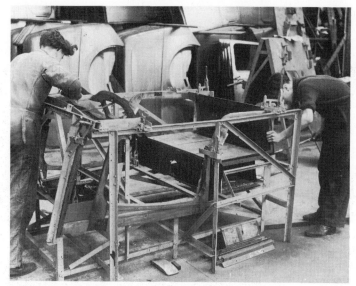

Initial assembly of a TD Midget body centre-section in the jig at the Morris Bodies Branch in Coventry. The very simple jigging, and the wooden frames, show how simple was the body of a Midget, and why it was so easy to reshape and restyle the cars without incurring huge costs.

Number sequence XPAG/TD2/9408 onwards.

Later, in 1952, there were other changes. From Engine Number 14224 a new type of combined engine-oil-filter body and pump housing was introduced, which is hardly significant, but from Engine Number 14948 the sump pan was increased from 9 pints to 10.5 pints, which should be of great interest to all those using their TDs in rallies, gymkhanas and races. Improved cylinder-block water circulation (and a new head gasket to suit the relocated holes in the block) was introduced from Engine Number 17968.

At Chassis Number 22251, the cable clutch linkage was replaced by a rod linkage, which was more for production convenience and reliability than an engineering improvement. Last, and by no means least (though it had no noticeable effect on the engine's performance), there was a new camshaft profile,

A near-complete and painted MG TD centre body section at the Morris Bodies Branch in Coventry. It is identifiable as a TD by the open battery box on the bulkhead, and by the provision for wipers and the wiper motor on the screen rail. In the background is a series of RM-type Riley body shells, also destined for transportation to Abingdon for final assembly.

The TD II production car, which came into existence as from Engine Number (*not* Chassis Number) 9408, began to be built in August 1951, and the improvements were confined to the engine and transmission. As from that number, the power train was fitted with an 8in diameter clutch (in place of the original 7.25in item) which necessitated changes to the flywheel and gearbox housings to accommodate the bigger clutch and the new thrust race; the diameter of the clutch withdrawal-fork shaft was increased from 0.625in to 0.75in at the same point.

It follows that although the TD II transmission was *potentially* capable of transmitting rather more torque than before, and was altogether more robust, the engines fitted were no more powerful than they had ever been. Do not let any owner of a TD II who is trying to sell you his car convince you otherwise. Original engines carried the Engine Number sequence XPAG/TD/501 up to XPAG/TD/9407, and later cars carried the Engine

Compared with that of the TC, the TD's facia and instrument panel layout was more logically designed. For the TD (though not, surprisingly, for the TF which would follow), the speedometer and matching rev-counter were always placed behind the steering wheel, whether that wheel was placed for left-hand or right-hand drive. A nice little touch on this MG facia was the provision for a two-pin plug (for a map-reading lamp power feed, perhaps) on the centre panel. Even in the early-1950s, however, there was no provision for a built-in heater, nor for a radio.

introduced from Engine Number 24116. The original timing (11-57-52-24 degrees in the usual nomenclature) had denoted a 35-degrees overlap around Top Dead Centre, and was linked to a recommended tappet clearance of 0.019in (hot). The overlap, incidentally, had been a feature of the TA and TC engines as well. The modified camshaft profile, which was also to be used on all TF models, had timing of 5-45-45-5 degrees — with only 10 degrees of overlap — and a recommended clearance of 0.012in (hot).

It is important to realize that the effective performance of the two profiles is the same, though the later profile is rather more refined and makes for a quieter engine. The mating of one particular profile to the tappet clearances recommended for it is important; the cam-lift and valve-spring details are the same for either camshaft.

As the TD was much the most numerous of all T-Series sports cars, it is the one most freely available to enthusiasts these days, especially in North America, where the majority of the cars were originally delivered. I recommend that you study closely Appendix C of this book, which details the number of cars built in each year, and the numbers delivered to each major market. When looking over a car which you might be considering buy-

In side view, the original TD Midget was not dramatically different from the TC, though it was somewhat more squat and was immediately recognizable by its smaller (15in) pressed-steel disc wheels. The fuel tank was less of an upright slab than before, and the spare wheel was more raked, to give a rather more sleek look to the shape.

At first it was strange to see an MG Midget fitted with bumpers, but the casual parking habits of North American customers, if for no other reason, made this innovation essential. In general style, however, the TD followed the lines of the TC, and the more complex independent front suspension is barely visible.

By a study of the known Chassis Number sequences, and of the numbers built in each year, I can also state the following with some confidence:

Year of manufacture	First Chassis Number	Final Chassis Number
1949	0251	0349
1950	0350	5116
1951	5117	12567
1952	12568	23405
1953	23406	29915

Not only did the TD have disc wheels (made very obvious by the external mounting of the spare wheel), but the hood had a single pane of celluloid to improve the rearward vision somewhat. This was a left-hand-drive machine destined for export, and the perforations in the wheels are those standardized quite early in the life of the TD.

ing, it is worth noting that Chassis Numbers started from 0251, while Engine Numbers started from 0501, and the two numbers on your car will most certainly *not* coincide. Just to confuse matters, it is also worth noting that a TD II in North America was known as a TDC!

These are the related chassis, engine and datal sequences which matter:

Chassis Number	Engine Number	Dates built
TD0251–TD9158	XPAG/TD/501– XPAG/TD/9407	November 1949– August 1951
TD9159–TD29915	XPAG/TD2/9408 onwards	August 1951– September 1953

Apart from its more square, squat style, with greater width across the passenger compartment, there were many obvious detail differences between TC and TD models, not least of which was the specification, for the very first time on a two-seater MG sports car, of chromium-plated bumpers. There were, of course, steel disc wheels (and a spare nave plate on the spare!), and a square numberplate holder. Rear visibility was still rather restricted.

As with previous T-Series models, the TD retained a one-piece backrest to its seat, but the width across the car was increased by a further four inches compared with the TC. When compared with the slim TA, therefore, the TD felt positively spacious. In modern times, no doubt, every safety-conscious country would reject a car like this, where the wiper motor was fixed to the inside of the windscreen, ideally placed to damage the passenger's head if he was jerked sharply forward in an accident.

The TD's peak year was 1952, which is very significant as it was achieved with virtually no competition from other British rivals. For 1953, however, demand was already seen to be turning down, and there was the threat from both Triumph and Austin-Healey, who had new models which looked more modern and carried attractive prices. It is now well-documented history that John Thornley and Syd Enever realized this at Abingdon in good time, and that they devised a new chassis and body style (EX175 — which later became that of the MGA production car) for approval by Sir Leonard Lord, who was the boss of their new masters, the British Motor Corporation. That this project was turned down at the time, and the TF was produced instead, forms the basis of the next chapter.

A carefully graduated series of 'Stage by Stage' tuning kits were available for TD models, and for such additional kits an extra set of Andrex suspension dampers, installed as shown on this car, were fitted. The main body of the damper was fitted to the car's bottom wishbones, with a link from the lever-arm being taken up to the chassis member supporting the main damper. It increased the unsprung weight a little, but not by enough to upset the overall handling balance.

This illustration is used to show that the installation of 'Stage' tuning Andrex dampers on the bottom wishbones was quite obvious. This car, too, has the perforated wheel discs introduced after less than a year of MG TD production.

CHAPTER 6

TF1250 and TF1500

1953 to 1955

Like every other model in the long-running MG T-Series family of sports cars, the TF evolved in a tearing hurry. Note that I do not say that it was 'developed', because this would be to exaggerate an altogether less sophisticated process. We know, from interviews with contemporary MG designers and staff, that the TF was derived from the current TD in no more than two weeks, with no mechanical changes of significance, and with no initial drawings being prepared at Cowley. The delay in translating the single hastily-built prototype into a production machine was caused by the need to draw what had already been made, and to have tools and patterns made!

Like the original TA, and the TD which was then in production, the TF was not the MG sports car which John Thornley and Syd Enever wanted to produce, but it was the only model they were allowed to put on sale by their financial and business masters. Since the beginning of 1952, of course, the Nuffield Group had been submerged into the new British Motor Corporation (B.M.C.), of which Len Lord was the undisputed master — and a more decisive and abrasive character than Lord Nuffield had ever been. It was Len Lord who had already chosen to have the new Austin-Healey 100 produced at Longbridge, and who had rejected MG's own new project, EX175, with which it was broadly similar.

The shock of EX175's rejection left Thornley and Enever numb for a short period, and the single prototype had to be stored away, even though they both felt that eventually it must rise to prominence again to become an important MG production model. However, even before the end of 1952, they received further depressing news — that demand for MGs in the United States (by far the most important market for MG sports cars) was beginning to fall away; dealers and potential customers, having seen that the square-rigged TD was to continue unchanged into its fourth year of production, were ordering fewer cars for delivery in 1953. Although the slump was neither as sudden, nor as alarming, as some other writers have suggested, it was still a noticeable and worrying decline.

In the winter of 1952–53, therefore, Thornley and Enever moved very swiftly to produce a 'facelifted' TD, which would be obviously different in its styling, but would not need lots of capital to be spent on new tooling — simply because the capital was not to be made available, and the luxury of time spent in making new tools was not there. Above all — and this affected the design process just as surely as any financial constraint — was the need to have the new model ready for display at the Earls Court Motor Show in October 1953, with deliveries beginning at once. Even then, due to the 'pipeline effect' of transporting cars in bulk to North America, sales in the United States would not begin until 1954.

There was no way in which any significant changes could be made to the chassis and running gear, so the new car used what was effectively the last variety of TD II mechanical components, allied to a Mark 2 type of tune for the 1,250cc XPAG engine, giving peak power of 57bhp at 5,500rpm with a compression ratio of 8.0:1. Although the same gearbox was retained, the final-drive ratio was raised to 4.875:1 (although the overall gearing was still more 'fussy' than that of the TA, TB and TC models).

Most welcome of all was that, after an interval of four years,

Produced as early as 1952 at a time when the TD Midget was still in production at Abingdon, this was the EX175 prototype, registered HMO 6, which was MG's entry for the unofficial 'design competition' sparked off by Len Lord in 1952, when he was looking for a future quantity-production sports car to be built by BMC. Although the TD's 1.25-litre engine, gear-box and back axle, along with the front suspension, were all used, EX175 had an entirely new chassis frame designed by Syd Enever. The bonnet hump was needed to clear the TD's rocker cover. Only one car was built, and at the time the project was rejected, but in all major respects this formed the basis of the MGA model which finally replaced the TF in 1955.

centre-lock wire wheels were once again to be available on an MG sports car, though the TD type of perforated disc wheels would still be standard equipment; as you would expect, these extras were very popular and were fitted to many examples.

What was the new car to be called? After the use of TA, TB, TC and TD, logic suggested that the new car should be a TE, but the schoolboy-humour connotations of 'Tee-Hee' ruled that out straight away. From there it was a simple step down the alphabet to arrive at the TF title, which was immediately adopted.

The centre-section of the new car's body shell — scuttle, doors and rear corners, was virtually unchanged, so that Morris Bodies in Coventry could readily adapt to making the revised car without delay. The most significant change, done in the interests of sleekness and to ally the new car with the monocoque MG Magnette which Gerald Palmer had designed at Cowley around B.M.C. components, and which was also to go into production at Abingdon by the end of 1953, was to adopt a sloping radiator style. Not only was this an innovation guaranteed to shock MG traditionalists (all previous MGs except the racing cars had had proudly vertical radiators), but it was a fake radiator at that. For the first time, an MG sports car was to have its real radiator hidden away behind a decorative grille.

The top of that radiator shell was 3½in lower than the TD's

radiator had been, which allowed the bonnet line to slope markedly forwards and encouraged newly styled front wings to be produced, which for the first time included fairings for the sealed-beam head-lamps. That was quite acceptable (and is now looked upon as a feature of some beauty), but no one had a good word for the new engine-access arrangements. For the first time (and this was a definite step backwards) the bonnet side panels were fixed and engine-bay access was somewhat limited. The use of pancake carburettor air cleaners was one result of this change, and although engine noise was hardly top of MG's problem areas it is a fact that the TF's intake noise was more pronounced than that of the TD.

At the rear there was a new and more sloping petrol tank (of 12-gallons capacity — slightly smaller than that of the TD and considerably smaller than the original TA's, which had 15 gallons) and swept wings more in keeping with this new style of car. The net result was that the TF was 2in longer overall than the TD, 1in wider due to more flamboyant wing styles, and perhaps ½in lower due to the revised hood and hood-iron shapes.

Welcome innovations included the use of individually adjustable seats (the common backrest of the other T-Types was finally discarded), the standardization of flashing direction indicators (not fitted to TDs for every market), and the provision of a map-reading lamp in the cockpit, which was going to be very useful for owners using their TFs in night rallies. At long last, Abingdon followed the lead given by Tickford in 1938 by fitting their TF's windscreen-wiper motor under cover behind the facia, and pivoted the wiper blades from the base of the screen; gone, therefore, was the potentially lethal mounting of the windscreen-wiper motor on the screen rail where it could be so injurious to a passenger's head. The windscreen, however, could still be folded flat in spite of the new wiper arrangements.

One definitely retrograde step was the location of instruments in the centre of the facia panel. On the TD, at least, the speedometer and rev-counter had been ahead of the driver's eyes, while even on earlier T-Series cars the rev-counter had faced him. On the TF, however, there was a cluster of instruments hiding behind octagonal surrounds, with rev-counter and speedometer separated by the auxiliary instruments. MG's only concession to function was that the rev-counter was nearest to the driver's line of sight, and swopped sides with the speedometer to accord with the steering-wheel position. But still,

From this angle, the fact that this is a TF, rather than a TD, rolling chassis is obvious from the shape and location of the radiator grille, though the layout of the carburation is also a good clue. TFs were in production from the autumn of 1953 to the late-spring of 1955.

As ready for installation in the TF, the combination of XPAG engine and its matching gearbox is virtually that of the previous Mark II version of the MG TD. An interesting but tiny detail difference is that the rocker/pushrod clearances are now advertised on this engine as 0.012in, whereas they were 0.019in on earlier examples.

The TF engine/gearbox looked very similar to the TD II except that a pair of pancake air-cleaners were fixed direct to the SU carburettors, and there was no cast-alloy trunking to a remote cleaner.

after all these years, there was no fuel gauge!

After the one and only TF prototype had been built — hardly designed — by Syd Enever's tiny development department at Abingdon, it was driven by John Thornley, speedily approved, and the wheels were set in motion to get it on sale. The drawing process took six months, and provision of production items like the new instruments, electrical accessories and revised body panels took even longer.

The last of the TDs — nearly 30,000 had eventually been built in 46 months — was produced in September 1953 and the first of the TFs followed in the next few days. The car was revealed to the world in the week before the Earls Court Motor Show and received a less than rapturous reception. This, however, was not nearly as derisive as some MG historians have suggested — their comments almost border on the hysterical — but there can be no doubt that it was not the MG which many observers wanted to see. This came as no surprise to MG management, because they thought so too!

Smart, neat, and — in its own way — stylish, but by the fashions of the early-1950s it was way behind the times, for the public had lost its taste for traditional sports cars. The centre-section, doors and general layout were unchanged, but both nose and tail were substantially altered. For the first time on an MG sports car the traditional type of radiator was in a semi-reclining position, and the headlamps were semi-faired into the wings. At last, thank goodness, wirespoke wheels were available again on a Midget.

From the tail, the TF's restyling is obvious. The spare wheel, the fuel tank profile and the line of the rear wings are all more flaring than before. It is noticeable that there are fewer louvres at the side of the engine bay, and the car now had fixed 'bonnet' sides, which made access to the TF's engine rather more difficult.

Having reverted to sanity and convenience for the TD, MG now produced the TF, where the same instrument panel was used, with centre-mounted instruments, whether right-hand or left-hand steering was ordered. This might have been convenient for the production planners, component buyers and company accountants, but it was not liked by the customers, as the rev-counter was no longer directly in front of their eyes. New on a Midget was the indicator switch (here almost hidden under the rim of the steering wheel) and for the first time in years the instrument bezels had octagonal shapes.

The fact that a TF is now usually looked on as the most graceful, and therefore the most desirable, of the T-Series models among classic-car enthusiasts may be a more balanced judgment. A glance at contemporary British magazines tells us a lot. *The Autocar* thought that 'the bodywork of . . . the recently introduced TF model has been restyled to produce a much cleaner external appearance though retaining the MG Midget characteristics', while *The Motor* commented that 'the MG Midget open sports 2-seater has been very much improved for 1954'. Britain's sporting weekly, *Autosport*, was less happy, pointing out that 'the TF is . . . built for the non-competition-minded class of purchaser, which, it must be admitted, forms the bulk of the small-capacity sports car users'.

The problem with the TF, on announcement, was not so much its looks, but its lack of significant performance improvements and its price. In the United States, for 1954, it was placarded at $2,250, which was $135 more than the TD which it displaced (though old-stock TDs sold in 1954 were only $105 cheaper) and $110 less than the TD Mark 2 which had the same engine tune. Here at home it was priced at £550 (basic), just £20 more than the last of the TDs.

These prices were reasonable enough by previous MG standards, but the problem now was that the Abingdon product was faced with serious and determined opposition — notably from Triumph's new TR2 and the Austin-Healey 100. The Austin-Healey 100 was undeniably very pretty, while the TR2 was certainly more attractive than those hysterical MG historians would have us believe, and both, at least, had smooth full-width styling appropriate to the 1950s. The bad news for MG was not only that both these cars were capable of more than 100mph when flat-out, when the TF's barn-door aerodynamics limited it to little more than 80mph, but that they were being offered at such bargain prices. The TF's direct competitor was the TR2, which had gone on limited sale in August 1953 for £555 (basic), while the Austin-Healey 100, with its 2.6-litre engine, was being retailed at £750 (basic). If the Austin-Healey 100 was not a direct rival on price grounds, it was certainly something which appealed strongly to North American buyers.

In the autumn of 1953, however, the production workforce at Abingdon were far too busy to worry about such things, as something of an all-change operation was in progress. Not only were they replacing the TD with the TF, but the Riley 2½-litre and MG YB saloons were being phased-out, substantial modifications were being made to the Riley 1½-litre saloons, the monocoque MG Magnette saloon was being started-up, and preparations were going ahead to build the new Riley Pathfinder. It was not only the disappointment of potential MG sports-car customers, but the sheer aggravation of making these monumental changes, which caused Abingdon's production achievement to fall away during the winter of 1953–54.

However, there was no doubt that the TF was a disappointment to many people, if only because it was quite obviously too slow and too old-fashioned. The great North American interest in traditionally-styled MGs was fading fast from that magnificent TD-inspired peak of 1952, and the TF was struggling. Like the TD, it relied so much on export sales for survival (only 5.5 per cent of all TDs built were sold in Britain), and those markets were turning against it; by the autumn of 1953, 1,542 of the 1,620 TFs built had been exported (95 per cent), but in 1954 that figure would sag to 85 per cent as total sales slumped. From 1945 to 1952 MG sales had consistently soared; until 1955, and the arrival of the MGA, they fell right away. By 1955 MG production would be back down to the TC-inspired levels of 1949.

Mechanically, the TF was very reliable and felt good to drive. The roadholding and handling (though somewhat soft for traditional tastes) were beyond reproach. No doubt most people would have forgiven the half-modernized looks if only the car had been fast enough, but that was the problem. With a maximum speed of little more than 80mph, and acceleration let down by a combination of the 57bhp power output and a two-up weight of 2,400lb, the TF was almost embarrassingly slow. It was no coincidence that the B.M.C. press office never allowed a TF to be tested by a British motoring magazine, and it must have been a source of anguish to learn that *Road and Track*, the influential North American motoring magazine, were able to test a TF with the 1,250cc engine for a spring-1954 issue. Those figures are reproduced in Appendix D, and tell their own story.

It was then that the nasty, slick, cruel phrases started to circulate. Tom McCahill commented 'Mrs Casey's dead cat, slightly warmed over'. Another comment was that it looked like a TD which had been kicked in the face. *Road and Track*, on the other hand, stated quite baldly that 'the new TF is an anomaly — a retrogression . . .'. But for all that they also commented that 'the fact remains that the entire staff of *R & T* vied with each other to produce the best reason for using the MG'.

B.M.C. and MG needed no more proof that the original TF was not good enough for the customer. It is well known, of course, that they started to produce the revised MG TF1500 in November 1954, but it is nonsense to suggest that this engine was developed from scratch *after* the problems were identified; even in the 1950s this would simply not have been possible. The larger 1,466cc engine, which was used in the EX179 record car in the summer of 1954, had been under development by the Morris Engines Branch in Coventry for a couple of years, even though the XP engine series was no longer a vital component in B.M.C.'s forward-planning.

It was, however, the only quick (as usual in the case of T-Series MGs) and simple way of making improvements to the T-Series sports car. During 1954, therefore, work to finalize the road-car tune for this engine was rushed through, so that it could speedily be put into quantity production at Coventry. The new engine — to be coded XPEG instead of XPAG (E stood for . . . Enlarged? . . . Who knows — all records have now been lost) was enlarged to 1,466cc, by what sounded like the simple expedient of providing a larger cylinder bore and 72mm pistons. The change, however, was much more difficult than that, as MG tuners had already discovered. With a standard 1,250cc block there was not enough metal thickness surrounding the bores to allow a straight bore increase of 5.5mm (0.216in) to be carried out with certainty. For race engines, where boring through into the water jacket could be corrected by the fitment of steel liners, the risk could be taken; for production units, a new and re-cored type of cylinder-block was

For some unaccountable reason this MG TF is fitted with Dunlop racing tyres, for not many TFs were ever fast enough to justify having them fitted. The nose style is undoubtedly neater and more integrated than that of the MG TD, as it has its sealed-beam headlamps partly faired into a modified front wing, and the electric wipers are now pivoted from the base of the screen and have hidden motors. The fixed 'bonnet' sides are more obvious in this view.

needed to achieve such an increase.

The problem, though, as already made clear in Chapter 2, was that the XPAG 1,250cc engine was already an enlargement of the original 1,140cc Morris 10 Series M unit, and was not intended to accommodate any more capacity 'stretch'. The solution for Morris Engines was to take, for them, the drastic step of using siamezed cylinder bores; although there was cooling water all round the cylinders of the 66.5mm-bore XPAG

engine, the larger-diameter bores for the XPEG unit could only be achieved by re-coring the cylinder-block casting and joining together each end pair of cylinders. Looked at from the 1980s, when such arrangements are commonplace, even on brand new engine designs, one wonders what the fuss was about, but I must point out that in 1953–54 the Morris Engines Branch had never before tackled what, to them, seemed like a revolutionary process. As we know, this was a satisfactory solution, and has since

One new feature about the TF, but not immediately obvious, was the provision of combined stop/tail/indicator lamps on the rear wings, now applied to home-market cars as well as to those intended for some export territories. On this particular car, the optional luggage tray is fitted — an important and popular accessory as stowage space behind the seats was somewhat limited.

been adapted to millions of other Morris/Austin and B.M.C./Leyland engines.

Externally, there were no visual clues (except, of course, for the Engine Numbers) that the XPEG engine was internally different and more powerful; the only significant cylinder-head change was to enlarge the combustion chambers to make sure that the compression ratio did not become unacceptably high due to the increased capacity. The improvement, incidentally,

was almost exactly in line with that expected from an enlargement without attention to breathing and camshaft profile. The capacity was increased by 17 per cent, as was the peak torque figure, while the peak power output rose by only 10 per cent.

By the autumn of 1954 the first TF1500 engines were ready, and during November of that year they were gradually fed into the production lines at Abingdon. Confusingly enough for historians, restorers and proud owners, there was no simple and decisive changeover from TF1250 to TF1500. At Chassis Number 6500 a change was made to the first 150 TF1500s, but this was followed by another 100 TF1250s, a further 100 TF1500s and a final 100 TF1250s before uninterrupted TF1500 production began at Chassis Number 6951.

It was a measure of the importance which MG attached to the North American market that almost every TF1500 was destined for sale over there and that the model was never sold in Great Britain; British buyers — who were never told more than the barest details of the existence of the revised model — had to make do with old stocks of TF1250s, or do without! It is also a measure of MG's desperation to keep sales up that they lowered the price of the TF1500 by no less than 11 per cent by comparison with the TF1250 — from $2,250 to $1,995.

It was a good try, but it did not work out. The TR2, in particular, had gained its North American foothold by then (and something of a rugged no-nonsense competitions reputation), and the great TR3 sales bonanza was about to take off. *Road and Track*'s retest of the TF1500, which started by quoting the phrase 'too little, too late, so what?' — even if they instantly qualified and rejected it — could do nothing to reassure the erstwhile MG fans. The TF1500 only achieved a mean top speed

A special two-seater coupe bodyshell built by Shipsides, the BMC dealers in Nottingham, on the basis of a TF chassis. There was a touch of MG Magnette (Palmer-style, 1953) or even of Standard Vanguard in the design, which never went into quantity production.

This new shape for an MG Midget sports car was proposed by Nuffield chief designer Gerald Palmer in 1953, even before the TF had been launched. His view was that if there was controversy about traditional or modern styling, it ought to be possible to offer two styles on the same TD/TF chassis. He suggested that this car could be the 'modern' style and that rather than have a completely welded-up steel body, it should have bolt-on skin panels attached to a common body base which could be modified to . . .

. . . the alternative more traditional shape shown here, which had different wings, doors, and — in this case — 'running boards'. It was an ingenious solution to a problem that, at the time, was critical to MG's future. However, the TF was introduced instead.

of 85.4mph, and it still needed 16.3 seconds to reach 60mph from rest (when a TR2 could do it in 12 seconds *and* beat the TF's fuel economy by 10mpg).

By then, however, MG had already lost interest in the TF as its replacement was on the way. The disasters which had overcome the MG marque during the first two years of B.M.C. rule persuaded Len Lord that he could do no worse by restoring their design autonomy and independence. In June 1954, therefore — five months before the TF1500 was even put on the market — the decision was made to re-open the Abingdon design office, and approval was given for an entirely new MG sports car, to be built on the basis of EX175.

The new car — to become the MGA, which was, and remains, no less famous than the T-Series models — had virtually nothing in common with the TF except for the front suspension. It was meant to be ready for production in June 1955, following an initial publicity launch in the Le Mans 24-Hours sports car race, and for that reason it was decided to stop production of TF1500s

at Abingdon in May. In the event, there were delays in preparing the body shells (from Morris Bodies Branch, Coventry), and no MG sports cars were built at Abingdon between June and August 1955 — the first hiatus of any length which had occurred since the company moved into residence at the end of 1929.

Between October 1953 and November 1954 a total of 6,200 TF1250s were built (an average of about 500 a month allowing for the phased change-over period), while between November 1954 and May 1955 they were followed by 3,400 TF1500s (a rate of rather more than 600 a month).

When the last TF1500 — Chassis Number TF10100 and Engine Number XPEG3940 — rolled off the simple brick assembly line at Abingdon, it brought to an end no less than 19 years of MG T-Series production, spanning five models. However, it was not quite the end of the line for the Morris-based XP engine family, which had been used in the Wolseley 4/44 saloons (in detuned form) since late-1952, should have been fitted to the 1953 MG Magnette if Gerald Palmer had had his way (Len Lord

This is the facia and provisional control layout of the 'Palmer prototype', which used instruments intended for the TF in a restyled cluster, and sensibly mounted directly ahead of the driver's eyes.

Ava atque vale. The car which replaced the TF in 1955 was the equally world-famous MGA, of which more than 100,000 were to be built before it was, in turn, replaced by the long-running MGB in the autumn of 1962. The only feature of the TF to be used once again in the MGA was the Issigonis-designed coil-spring front suspension. Everything else — chassis frame, body shell, engine, transmission and back axle — were new to MG.

insisted otherwise) and was to be used until the last of the 4/44s was built in the spring of 1956.

In every way, it was the end of an era for MG, and for B.M.C. Many components (in modern terms we call then 'building blocks') like the engine, gearbox and back axle no longer had a place in the ruthless rationalization scheme being pushed through by B.M.C. from Longbridge; the planners were happy to see them go.

The XPAG/XPEG engine had been fitted to MGs since 1939, and the gearbox (in one form or another) since 1936. The hypoid-bevel axle had been new for the MG TD of 1950, though was shared with earlier Nuffield production cars.

There would be a place for separate steel chassis frames in MGs of the future (the MGA would use one until 1962), but the TF had the last of the coachbuilt body shells. The Magnette saloon was pressed-steel, and other coachbuilt shells from the Morris Bodies Branch (the Riley 1½-litres, for instance) were also being phased-out. There was not an ounce of structural wood in the MGA's shell, nor in future MG sports cars.

The style, too, was dead, for no further traditionally-styled sports cars would ever be built at Abingdon. Surprisingly enough, however, the 'bug-eyed' Austin-Healey Sprite of 1958 carried more than a hint of the old TF in the way its head-lamps were mounted ahead of curving nacelles.

Finally, of course, with the last of the TFs we saw the end of the model name Midget, 27 years after it had first been used on the M-Type of 1928. There was nothing 'Midget' about the MGA, and it would not be until 1961 that a badge-engineered Austin-Healey Sprite would appear, carrying the Midget brand name.

When MG enthusiasts saw the new MGA they split into two groups. There were those who embraced the new shape, style and philosophy with open arms. The other (and who is to say now that they were wrong) looked sadly at the new car and wondered if MGs had finally lost their charm. Which group was right?

CHAPTER 7

TD and TF in competition

Le Mans, Silverstone and record-breaking

Between 1950 and 1954, during the greater part of the production run of the TD and TF models, there was no Competitions Department at Abingdon. Furthermore, Nuffield (later, B.M.C.) policy actively discouraged MG from offering obvious material and financial support to their private owners. Indeed, if I was to limit this section to a survey of the works-sponsored TDs and TFs which retained their standard bodywork it would be very short. It was only in 1955, when the last batch of MG TF1500s was being built, that the new B.M.C. Competitions Department was opened at Abingdon. The team only used TFs once or twice (for Pat Moss, Stirling's sister) and they achieved little success.

MG management, however, was resourceful enough in finding ways of giving behind-the-scenes support for some racing programmes in the British Isles, to devise special bodywork for a private Le Mans effort and to organize three series of record-breaking expeditions to the salt flats at Utah with two different MG record cars. Last, and by no means least, the engineers at Abingdon developed a whole range of 'Stage' tuning kits, so that private owners could boost the performance of their XPAG engines.

Chronologically, therefore, I must start this section with a note about the works-sponsored TDs which raced in Great Britain and Northern Ireland in 1950 and 1951. This story really starts with the Abingdon-prepared TCs already described in Chapter 4, for it was in 1949 that one of the drivers involved with those cars, George Phillips, first spotted a prototype TD during a visit to Abingdon, pressed for a drive and was offered a trial run. That run, and a further trial by Dick Jacobs in company with John Thornley, led to many suggestions being made for performance improvements.

Some of these (including improved suspension and better ventilation to the brakes by means of perforated wheels) were incorporated into one car, which was registered FMO 885 (which still exists) and was loaned to Dick Jacobs for a production car race at Blandford Camp, in Dorset. Jacobs was delighted to finish first in this event in front of 1½-litre HRGs which were nominally faster but had inferior brakes. However, the MG had extra Andrex dampers fitted to its front suspension, and these were declared non-standard (which, indeed, they were) by the organizers, who awarded first prize to an HRG.

As a direct result of this performance, Abingdon catalogued a new version of the TD known as the TD Mark 2, and decided to build a team of three new cars to take part in the Silverstone production car race, and the International Tourist Trophy race at Dundrod, in Northern Ireland. The new cars — FRX 941, FRX 942 and FRX 943, to be driven by Dick Jacobs, George Phillips and Ted Lund respectively — were no quicker than the 1949 TCs when first used at Silverstone, but they put up a very creditable performance in the race. Although Gerry Ruddock's 1½-litre HRG proved to be too fast for the 1¼-litre MG TDs, all three works cars finished strongly, second, third and fourth in that class. Dick Jacobs' car, which finished second, averaged 71.27mph, which was a significant improvement on the pace of the 1949 TC in the previous event.

For the T.T. the full 'Mark 2' tune was approved by the authorities, which meant that the cars could now use not only the 1½in SU carburettors, but also the 9.3:1 compression ratio.

The same three cars were entered for the T.T. with the original (Blandford) car taken along as the team's spare. In this race, of course, the TDs would not only have to mix it with similar production cars, but also with the very fastest machines like the new XK120 Jaguars, which were being driven by stars like Stirling Moss and Peter Whitehead. Since these cars were at least a full minute quicker than the TDs over a single lap, the drivers of the Abingdon cars would need to keep a wary eye on their rear-view mirrors at all times!

The T.T., however, was a three-hour race, where reliability would be as important a factor as performance, so the MG team was not at all downcast by their performance problems. The fact that it was raining hard throughout the race was also welcomed by the team, for this made the faster cars much more difficult to handle. After the first hour, with cars spinning off in all directions, the Abingdon-prepared TDs were in complete command of the 1½-litre class, with Jacobs, Lund and Phillips in first, second and third positions. All three cars continued undaunted for the rest of the race, and although the engine in Ted Lund's car ran short of oil and destroyed a big-end just two laps from the end, the cars still finished in first (Jacobs), second (Phillips) and third (Lund) positions, with Jacobs' car averaging 63.20mph. That speed sounds pedestrian until I compare it with that of the XK120 Jaguar which won in the hands of Stirling Moss, which only managed to average 75.15mph! Jacobs' car, incidentally, finished in 16th place overall.

For 1951, although MG were willing to support their drivers in these cars, they did not actually keep and prepare them at the factory. In the *Daily Express* production car race Dick Jacobs' ex-works car won the 1½-class at 72.66mph, which was another improvement compared with the 1950 times, and in doing so he set a fastest lap at 75.36mph. The really satisfying feature was

Oh, happy days! In 1949 a car intended for racing at the Le Mans 24-Hours race could also be used on the road and parked on the street in London! This was George Phillips' special-bodied MG TC, which he drove at Le Mans in 1949 and 1950. In 1949 the car was disqualified, but in 1950 Phillips took second place in his class, co-driven by Eric Winterbottom. As far as is known, this car is no longer in existence, but note the appropriate (and genuine) registration number!

In 1950, George Phillips (*Autosport's* chief photographer in later years) once again entered his special-bodied and highly-tuned MG TC for the Le Mans 24-Hours sports car race. Unlike his bad luck in 1949, the 1950 race went much as planned, and with co-driver Eric Winterbottom, Phillips drove the TC into 18th place and finished second in the capacity class behind the 1½-litre Jowett Jupiter driven by Tom Wisdom and Tommy Wise. Here is the gallant TC, pictured at White House. (*The Autocar*)

that he defeated Ruddock's HRG, which was a long way behind in second place, marginally slower than it had been in 1950.

In 1951, however, Abingdon's biggest effort went into support for George Phillips' Le Mans entry. In 1949 and again in 1950 the intrepid Phillips had entered a special TC at Le Mans, as described in Chapter 4. For 1951 MG development staff, led by Syd Enever, agreed to prepare a special car for him to drive, using an entirely new body on a race-tuned TD Mark 2 chassis.

This car, appropriately registered UMG 400, does not appear to have survived, but was enormously significant to MG's future plans. John Thornley and Syd Enever both realized that the classic, unaerodynamic shape of the TD was obsolete, and that the next generation of MGs would have sleek full-width styling.

Here, for Le Mans, was a chance to try-out their ideas of what the next cars might be.

Under the skin, UMG 400, or EX172, as it was defined in the list of MG experimental projects, was a fully race-prepared Mark 2 TD, retaining its perforated disc wheels and having a normally-aspirated 1,250cc XPAG engine and the normal TD gearbox and hypoid-bevel rear axle. The body shell, however, was an attractive new style, personally evolved by Syd Enever, who had studied all the good features in streamlining exhibited by the MG record car EX135. It was remarkably similar to the shape which would be adopted for the MGA project in future years; the shape, in fact, needed little basic change for the MGA as that car was to retain the same 7ft 10in wheelbase.

For 1951, MG built a special prototype car for George Phillips to drive in the Le Mans 24-Hours sports car race. In effect it was a complete race-tuned TD Mark II rolling chassis, on to which a sleek new body, designed by Syd Enever, had been fitted. This style, of course, later became the basis of the famous shape evolved for the MGA.

The cockpit of the 1951 Le Mans special version of the TD, driven by George Phillips, showing the use of octagonal speedometer and rev-counter styling which would later be adopted for the TF in 1953.

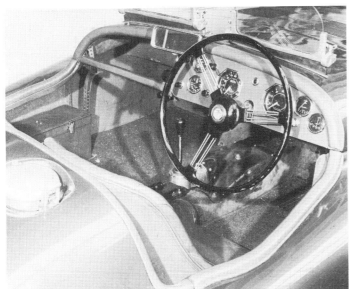

Phillips' problem, however, was that there was no way of lowering the driving seat, which sat uncompromisingly on top of the box-section TD chassis frame, and the major failing of this project was that he was forced to sit so high that he was barely protected by the aero screen. Even so, this race-prepared TD was capable of 120mph in a straight line.

It was the smallest-engined British entry that year, for which Phillips took along Alan Rippon as his second driver. In practice the car's engine gave trouble, due to the low-octane fuel supplied (which was inferior to the 80-octane brew normally supplied in Britain), and to cut down on the detonation an extra cylinder-head gasket was fitted to reduce the compression ratio.

In the race the car performed very well for three hours, but after 60 laps one of the heavy oversize inlet valves broke, went through the crown of a piston and immobilized the engine; co-driver Alan Rippon had not even had a chance to drive this interesting and attractive car.

No other T-Series cars were prepared or entered by the MG factory until 1955. At the beginning of that year, in a complete change of policy, B.M.C. had decided to re-open the Competitions Department at Abingdon, put Marcus Chambers in charge of its fortunes, directed that success was to be achieved, and stated that the money necessary to ensure this would be made available. It was a decision not unconnected with the fact that Healey and Triumph had both recently embarked on their own competition programmes, with considerable success.

Although the Competition Department's programme was mainly concentrated on the new MGA, and particularly on the Le Mans entry of three prototype EX182s (MGAs with light-alloy bodies), they took on a single MG TF1500, registered KRX 90, with which they began to enter Pat Moss in various events.

At the time, far too many people dismissed the redoubtable Miss Moss as a publicity gimmick for B.M.C., suggesting that she was being employed merely because she was Stirling's sister, not because she could drive a car fast. How wrong they all were! Before long Pat proved that she was not only the fastest lady driver in the world, but often as fast as the best men.

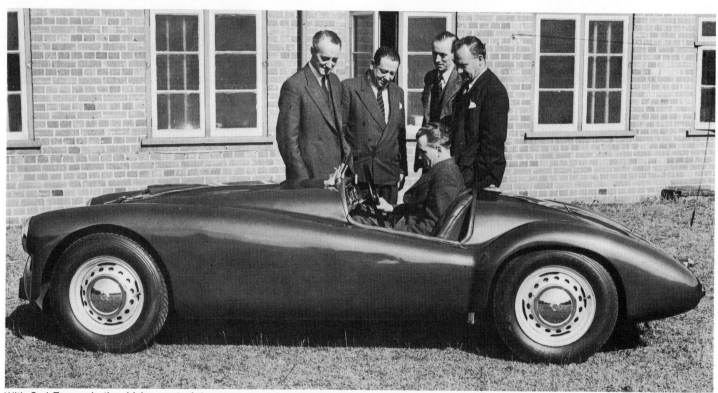

With Syd Enever in the driving seat of the 1951 special-bodied MG TD which competed at Le Mans, the low and sleek lines are obvious. Second from the right is John Thornley, who was in charge of MG's affairs for almost all of the 1950s and 1960s. Even though the TD's engine was race-tuned with a 24-hours race in mind, it was still powerful enough to push the car along at nearly 120 mph – or almost 40 mph more than the standard TD could achieve in 'over the counter' tune.

George Phillips' 'Le Mans special' MG TD, complete with MGA-style prototype body, competing in the 1951 Le Mans race with Phillips acknowledging the presence of *The Autocar*'s photographer. The bonnet scoop was to direct cool air direct to the carburettor air intakes. There can have been very little weather protection behind that single small aero screen, which might explain the reason for Phillips being so well wrapped up. The car only lasted three hours in the race, at which point an engine valve broke before co-driver Alan Rippon had a chance to drive. Such an engine failure was not unknown to TD racers at the time. (*The Autocar*)

In the TF1500, however, she had very little success, which perhaps shows that the car itself was not competitive. In the spring she was entered in a ladies' handicap race at Goodwood, which she won with some ease, but in the R.A.C. Rally of that year, which included a multitude of driving tests, and for which the weather was very wintry, she had little success. But then, even Ian Appleyard, who had twice won the event outright in his XK120, could only manage third place in class in his own TF1250 . . .

Pat, co-driven by Pat Faichney, finished third in the ladies' contest behind Sheila Van Damm's Sunbeam Mark 3 and Jo Ashfield's Ford Zephyr, but her car was completely outclassed by its lack of pace, and to rally it round Britain for five or six days in such weather must have been extremely uncomfortable. Apart from its use in one or two minor events there was no further involvement with the TF1500 after this, and from the end of the year the MGA became important, not only as a competition car, but as the mainstay of the production lines at Abingdon.

During the early-1950s, however, Abingdon once again became involved in the very specialized sport of record-breaking, first by supporting the venerable EX135, and later by building a new car, EX179. Although neither used the chassis of a T-Series production car, both used one or other versions of the XPAG engine and deserve description here.

EX135 is probably the most famous of all the MG record cars, for it took its first record in 1934 and its last in 1952. In that time it used a variety of engines, ranging from supercharged K3 Magnette units, sometimes with as many as four of the six cylinders put out of action, to prototype four-cylinder twin-cam Jaguar engines (when the car was not called an MG, but a Gardner Special) and much-modified six-cylinder Wolseley units, as well as XPAG engines.

Immediately after the war it had been bought by Lt Col 'Goldie' Gardner, who benefited from generous sponsorship from the Duckhams oil company. In its postwar form it used the off-set-transmission type of K3 chassis and the streamlined body shell designed and developed by Reid Railton at Thomson and Taylor's premises, and it had right-hand steering.

For 1951 Gardner had the car re-engined by MG, who took an active interest in the attempts, and put both Reg Jackson and Syd Enever on to the project 'in their spare time'. The aim was to set new marks in Class F (for cars of between 1,100cc and 1,500cc), from straight-line maximum speed attempts to those of one hour's duration, for which a circular track was to be used.

Two different 1,250cc XPAG engines were prepared, the 'sprint' unit being to a much higher state of tune than that to be used for the endurance runs. For short-distance maximum-speed runs up to 10 miles the XPAG unit was equipped with a Shorrock supercharger delivering no less than 25psi of boost and had a compression ratio of 9.3:1 (in other words the normal Stage tuning for a Mark 2 engine was retained), at which a staggering 210bhp was developed at 7,000rpm. By comparison, the endurance engine had a mere 10psi of boost, a compression ratio of 7.25:1 and a peak power output of 92bhp at 5,400rpm. After learning of those figures, no one surely could claim that the T-Series engines were less tunable than the overhead-camshaft units they had replaced?

The first part of the venture, the endurance running, was partly successful, with Gardner taking six new International Class F records at up to 137.4mph during the hour's run, but this part of the running then had to be abandoned when a fractured oil pipe led to an engine failure. The sprint section of the runs had to be abandoned, first because the timing equip-

Close racing at Silverstone in the production car race held at the International Trophy meeting in August 1950. There were three works-prepared (but privately entered) MG TDs in the event, driven by George Phillips, Ted Lund and Dick Jacobs. For much of the race the cars were scrapping with one or other of the 1½-litre HRGs, and swopped positions repeatedly. Here at Copse Corner, Ted Lund's car is ahead of Dick Jacobs, as both harry an HRG. Jacob's TD eventually finished second in the class (with Lund third and Phillips fourth) at a speed of 71.27 mph. (*The Autocar*)

ment broke down, and later because the weather changed and the salt track became waterlogged.

A year later Gardner and his old MG record car went back to Utah, not only with the XPAG supercharged engines, but with an alternative six-cylinder Wolseley-based engine of 1,973cc. It was his intention to raise his own Class F records, set new Class E records, and also attack the sprint records which had been abandoned in 1951. His Wolseley-engined attempts (Class E) came first, on the circular track, and although three new figures were set at distances up to 100 kilometres, unfortunately his car then spun at more than 150mph, demolishing a marker post and injuring the driver more seriously than he would admit.

With the MG engines installed, therefore, there was only time to take International Class F records for a flying 5 miles and 10 kilometres (the better figure being 189.5mph), and Gardner also achieved a one-way best speed of 202.14mph for the flying

kilometre, which did not count for International records as these had to be achieved in two directions. With the sprint engine installed, therefore, EX135 was almost exactly as fast on salt as it had been with the supercharged K3 Magnette engine on tarmac. The pity of it all, as far as lovers of the XPAG engine were concerned, was that EX135 was never given another chance to prove her outright best speed again, as Gardner retired immediately after this session.

In 1954 Captain George Eyston, who seems to have broken every record known to motoring man at one time or another, persuaded B.M.C. to have a new record car built, and because he was a director of Castrol he was able to arrange sponsorship from his own oil company. The new EX179, though outwardly similar to EX135, was different in almost every respect. Its chassis was a spare prototype frame from the EX175 (MGA) project, and it had left-hand drive. Into this structure, for 1954,

Early days in a very famous partnership – Pat Moss, Ann Wisdom and a BMC car – the combination which brought fame and success to the BMC team in so many events over the years. Pat's first event for BMC's works competitions department, which was based at Abingdon, was to take this TF – KRX90 (does it still survive?) – on the RAC International Rally. Later, she entered the car in the London MC's Little Rally, and is seen here rolling through a ford on the way to the start of a braking test. Then, as now, rally organizers had a very strange sense of humour!

107

a modified XPAG-type of engine was mated to the TD/TF gearbox, and drove through a special straight-cut differential.

This time, however, the engine was not supercharged. Instead, the occasion was used to prove the enlarged XPEG engine of 1,466cc, which was about to go into production in the TF1500. This unit boasted nothing more ambitious than twin 1¾in-choke SU carburettors, larger valves and a compression ratio of 10.7:1. As with EX135, short exhaust stubs curved up from the cylinder-head, and the exhaust was expelled through four tiny rectangular holes in the bonnet top above the engine. The peak power output was only 84bhp at 6,000rpm.

Thus equipped, George Eyston and the American-based driver Ken Miles took a further eight endurance records at Utah in August 1954, some already held by EX135, at speeds up to 153.69mph. It was a great vindication of MG's love of record-breaking, which brought great publicity dividends in markets

One of MG's most famous record cars, EX135, which evolved from the chassis and running gear of one of the 'off-set' K3 Magnettes of the 1930s. In 1951 EX135, by now known as the Gardner-MG, was re-engined yet again, this time with a 1.5-litre supercharged version of the MG TD's engine. The massive supercharger and the twin-SU carburettors are installed between the front dumb-irons, down in the nose and immediately behind the radiator. In this form the car captured six endurance records at speeds up to 137.4 mph. A year later, also driven by Goldie Gardner, it achieved 189.5 mph in a straight line during EX135's final racing appearance.

The last of MG's traditional type of record cars was EX179, which was built in 1954 and featured a prototype MGA chassis frame. The front suspension, wheels and much-modified XPEG MG TF 1.5-litre engine were all from the basic TF which was then in production. Driven at Utah by the late Captain George Eyston and the late Ken Miles, the car took eight endurance records at speeds up to 153.69 mph.

throughout the world, and proved that not only could their designers evolve very efficient wind-cheating bodies (even if their masters would not put them on sale!) but that they could also produce engines to run at high revolutions for hundreds of miles on end. Although EX179 was used on two more occasions, and later was re-engineered as EX219, it never made any more runs with an XPAG or XPEG engine installed. EX135, incidentally, has been preserved for all time in exhibition form, with perspex display panels let in to important areas of the bodywork, and the supercharged MG TF engine is still installed.

None of these exploits, of course, would have been significant to the MG sports car owner if the lessons learned had not eventually been passed on to them in the form of improved or optional equipment. But at MG, every operation of this kind had a commercial motive. For the XPAG family of engines a whole series of 'Stage' tuning kits was developed, and by 1950

these were all available. The 'bible' which listed them, their operation and their performance, was *Tuning for MG Midget Engines*, now long out of print, and surviving copies are real collectors' pieces for MG enthusiasts.

Five different stages of tune were made available, the most extreme featuring a Shorrock supercharger and 9.3:1 compression ratio, with peak power of 97bhp at 6,000rpm; to all intents and purposes, this was the endurance tune used in EX135 for the 1951 and 1952 record attempts. Here are the details of each of the stages, which might have been applied to a T-Series car you buy, or may be built into a spare engine you may be thinking of purchasing:

Stage 1 is a simple tune-up. The cylinder-head is machined (by 3/32in) to raise the compression ratio to a nominal 8.6:1, ports are polished, larger valves and stronger valve springs are fitted, 1½in SU carburettors are added and the resulting peak

The sleek lines of the 1954 MG record car, EX179, which was most easily distinguished from its close relative, EX135, by its left-hand driving position. In this original form it hid an unsupercharged 1,466 cc XPEG engine, whose short exhaust stacks poke up through the 'bonnet' panel.

power output is 60bhp at 5,600rpm. At the same time the axle ratio is raised from 5.125:1 to 4.875:1, and an extra pair of dampers — Andrex hydraulic lever-arm type — are fitted to the front suspension. These have their bodies clamped to the botton wishbones, and their arms are connected to the cross-member.

Stage 2 tuning is more ambitious, and required a 50 per cent alcohol fuel when announced, but now needs no more than the best premium fuel. The compression ratio is further raised to 9.3:1 by machining a further 1/32in from the head, fitting retuned 1½in SUs and liberating the very creditable total of 69bhp at 5,500rpm.

Stage 3 tuning was meant purely for motor racing, where the very best fuel was available. This featured a 12.0:1 compression ratio (a combination of standard cylinder-head and special pistons) and all the 'goodies' already mentioned. Peak power was 78bhp at 5,750 rpm, and it was usual to fit a 4.55:1 axle. Starting

from cold with a standard starter motor was extremely difficult, and it was usually recommended that a tow car or a group of strong and enthusiastic 'pushers' should be engaged instead!

Stage 4, the most ambitious road tune, combined the use of a standard engine and cylinder-head with a Shorrock supercharger drawing its air through a single 1½in SU carburettor. This gave a good deal more torque than the standard engine could produce, but with a fairly modest increase in peak power to 71bhp at 5,500 rpm. The blower gave only 6psi of boost and was belt-driven from the nose of the crankshaft.

Stage 5 combined a high-compression (9.3:1) cylinder-head and powerful Shorrock supercharging, although a single 1½in SU carburettor and 6psi of boost was all that was needed. It is a measure of the TD's aerodynamic problems that with a 4.55:1 axle ratio and with hood and sidescreens in position the maximum speed is still less than 100mph; even with a mere 68bhp in 1955, the MGA could beat this mark in only slightly favourable conditions.

The Autocar, which tested one car in all these different stages of tune, summed up the position perfectly by stating that a Stage 4 tune liberating an extra 17bhp was worth only 9.5mph, while the full-blooded Stage 5 competition tune with an extra 43bhp produced only an extra 23.5mph maximum speed. The fault was not with the engine, but with the aerodynamics. That MG felt able to release such information for the super-tuning of their XPAG engine — which, incidentally, involved no camshaft changes whatsoever — means that they were supremely confident of the ability of the unit to withstand a great deal of punishment. Considering that it had been developed from a design originally meant for nothing more ambitious than a 10hp (R.A.C. Rating) Morris and Wolseley model, this is remarkable.

Ever since then, MG enthusiasts have repeatedly blessed the engineers who built such hidden reserves into such a straightforward design. Even though the engine which replaced the XPAG/XPEG on the assembly lines — the B.M.C. B Series — also proved to be surprisingly tunable, it never gained so many fans. Perhaps this was because the XPAG/XPEG engines were the last which the MG enthusiasts would be willing to call 'MG' units. If indeed they were, they were engines of which Cecil Kimber would have been proud.

CHAPTER 8

Buying a T-Series MG

The choice, the examination and the road test

I will begin with one incontestable remark — that the youngest T-Series MG sports car not built from a box of spare parts (or completely rebuilt) is now at least 25 years old. Worse, the TA models are now well over 40 years old. That, if nothing else, should make you realize that you must judge the possible purchase of a T-Series car in an entirely different way from that applicable to a more recent thoroughbred, both as regards condition and the price you will have to pay.

It goes without saying, I hope, that there is no foolproof way to search for and find the T-Series car of your choice for enjoyment or regular use. It simply is not enough to go by the asking price, and I would emphatically not say that you must ignore certain types. I have seen far too many enormously expensive TFs which have included botched repair and restoration under a glossy skin, and I have also seen early T-Series cars sold, unrestored, at remarkably reasonable prices. All that this chapter can hope to achieve, therefore, is to provide you with a better idea of what is available, what is normal and what is most certainly not, and some of the pitfalls.

I am afraid that it is now too late to find and purchase a cheap T-Series model which you can use every day without spending a great deal of time and money on its preparation. In Great Britain and in North America the huge interest in recently-obsolete sporting and thoroughbred cars began to mushroom some years ago. All the real T-Series bargains were struck in the 1960s. The price asked for a T-Series sports car now, in the early-1980s, is set not so much by the intrinsic value of the machines, or their worth by comparison with their rivals, but because the phenomenon of investment has really struck home at these cars.

Be prepared, therefore, to pay what you may consider is a high price even today. Consider then if the fuel supply and price prospects for the 1980s and beyond may one day yield you a profit on selling. Or don't you intend to sell, ever?

If you go looking for a T-Series MG after reading this book, be prepared to be patient. If your live in Great Britain, North America, or the two old 'British Empire' territories of South Africa or Australasia, there should be quite a healthy market in most varieties of T-Series models. If you live in a country where very few T-Series cars were ever sold (which, surprisingly enough, includes several European countries) then you might be forced to wait for a very long time, or to buy a car which is neither the type, nor in the state of preservation, which you really wanted.

Throughout this book, so far, I have made passing mention of the number and destination of all new T-Series models built between 1936 and 1955. In Appendix C, however, I list this progress in tabular form, and I am confident that these statistics are accurate for the years 1945 to 1955. For the TA and TB models, however, I have no precise estimates of exports (although I understand that about 15 per cent of MG production went overseas in those years), nor of the year-on-year production of TA models.

All in all, however, it is easy enough to see what sort of T-Series model should be available, even today, allowing for unbalancing factors like the probability that the earlier models (TA, TB and TC) were decimated and allowed to be scrapped in a much more cavalier fashion than were the TDs and TFs of later years, and that there were fewer of them to start with.

There were 52,646 T-Series cars in all. Even if you take the surely pessimistic view that less than a third of them have survived, that still leaves a total of more than 15,000 T-Series cars extant in the world. That estimate, if nothing else, should

The partially assembled cylinder-block and details of the 1936–39 TA Midget engine showing the rather 'tall and thin' layout of the engine. MOWOG, of course, was a Nuffield tradename for parts supplied for MOrris, WOlseley and MG cars of the period. From the disposition of the cylinder bores, it is clear that this particular 1,292cc version of the famous '102mm stroke' engine has the smallest cylinder bore of the entire family. The VA 1½-litre model, for example, had larger bores and a capacity of 1,548cc, while competition versions could be enlarged still further to 1,708cc; in that case the bore was 73 mm, compared with 63.5 mm for the standard engine.

ensure that the selling price of cars which come on the market should never become prohibitive, and it should also make the continuing production of obsolete spare parts (by specialist concerns) a viable proposition.

Only 3,003 of these 52,646 cars were TAs, with the original MPJG long-stroke engine. Be realistic. Even though the MPJG was shared in many respects with the VA-Series MGs, there were only 2,407 of them, and *their* owners are also looking for spares! At least in respect of its engine, therefore, a TA will be more difficult to maintain or restore. I'm not saying it is impossible—the enthusiastic Morris clubs have good reason to keep up MP . . supplies for their own purpose—but it should lead you to think. For overseas readers I suspect that the TA is virtually unknown anyway, so this remark applies mainly to British T-Series enthusiasts.

Of all the T-Series models ever built, only 379 were TBs, built in 1939, but this is no disadvantage. The engine and gearbox was 'as TC', as was most of the chassis and running gear, while the body was of the narrow TA type, which is straightforward, if not cheap, to restore. Your rare TB (and, believe me, they *are* rare) is very desirable for that very reason. But if you are offered a TB about which you are suspicious, be sure to check the Chassis Numbers (which must begin with TB . . .) and the fact that the XPAG engine is matched to a narrow-style body and a chassis which includes trunnion supports to front and rear springs. (No one, surely, will have gone to the extent of *completely* rebuilding a TC to make a TB of it?) If you still have doubts, check through the various sources that your car has a 1939 registration number.

Of all the T-Series models, 13,382 were of the original TA/TB/TC type, with rigid-axle front and rear springs and the chassis pedigree of the original 1936 TA. This means that they accounted for only 25 per cent of the T-Series total, and because of the premature scrapping I mentioned earlier I doubt if more than 15 per cent of all survivors (or about 2,000 cars) are of this style. If you *must* have this sort of MG, therefore, be prepared to pay a high price, and probably to have a long wait to find the car you really want to own.

Apart from the normal two-seater open sports type of body shell built by Morris Bodies in large numbers, the only two other styles ever approved by MG were the Airline coupe

The robust 'bottom end' of the TA Midget's 1,292cc engine nevertheless shows that the crankshaft had no counterbalancing weights, which meant that it was not as easy to tune the unit for really high revolutions in competition form. Note that the sides of the cylinder-block extend well down below the centreline of the crankshaft.

offered for the TA in 1937 and 1938 and the smart Tickford drophead coupe of 1938 and 1939 available for the TA and TB. The Airline was built in such tiny numbers that no record of the quantity built has survived, neither, apparently, has such a car. There were more Tickford-bodied cars, and some of these have survived, are extremely rare and consequently both desirable and expensive. (Before its rarity value became recognized, one

member of the British MG Car Club actually bought an Airline model and had it rebuilt as a normal Abingdon-style two-seater; his teeth are still gnashing!)

Although the TD is considerably more numerous than the TF, and although the style of the TD is considered more 'pure' by disinterested observers, it is the TF which has the greater value on the enthusiast's market. This is astonishing as it was

This detail view of the cylinder-head and combustion chambers of the TA's engine forms an interesting comparison with that of the later TB/TC unit. This head, of course, was originally developed for use in the 10/40 and 12/48 Wolseleys which preceded the TA Midget by a short period, but it was later adopted for the Series III Morris 10s and 12s of the 1938 and 1939 model years.

the T-Series model which attracted the most criticism when it was current, and is the version which was found to be most lacking in performance by comparison with its rivals. Now, however, the rather shaved-down style seems to be more desirable than that of the TD. It follows, therefore, that a TD is a better bargain in terms of intrinsic value for money.

The so-called Mark 2 TDs were very rare, and the MG C.C. has supplied me with statistics to show that only 47 true competition cars were ever built. This is not to say, however, that no other cars were converted after original sale (some undoubtedly were), but it serves to show that the vast majority of all TDs were of the quantity-production type.

More details of the Abingdon-approved 'Stage' tuning kits are available in reprinted form in other MG publications, but it should be worth noting that each and every complete tuning kit included the fitting of Andrex (not Andre) lever-arm hydraulic shock absorbers to the front suspension. Note, too, that different axle ratios were specified for different kits; if you are looking at a modified car, make sure that the correct ratio is still in place. Checking it is simple enough.

Of the total of 9,600 TFs, there were 3,400 TF1500s with the enlarged XPEG 1,466cc engine — 35 per cent of the TF produc-

tion total. XPEG engines, therefore, make up less than 7 per cent of the total number of all XP . . engine types fitted to T-Series models, and although they are largely similar to the 1,250cc XPAG types it means that spare parts (particularly the special cylinder-blocks) are more difficult to find. Paradoxically, well over 7 per cent of the survivors have XPEG engines because they were the best liked type and were fitted to the last series of cars to be built.

A look at the table of performance figures in Appendix D, all of which are taken from independent sources and are not factory hand-out figures, shows that there was really very little improvement in T-Series performance over the years, which explains why press comments became more strident as the years passed by. I am deeply suspicious of the way in which *Road and Track* achieved acceleration figures considerably better than those achieved by *The Autocar*, for the very similar maximum speeds suggest that power outputs were the same. I know from personal experience that *The Autocar*'s figures were always taken with the aid of an accurate fifth-wheel speedometer and in two-passenger loading conditions, so I can only assume that *Road and Track* used different methods more favourable to the car.

However, it seems that only the TF1500 can be expected to beat 80mph in normal conditions without wind assistance and with the hood and sidescreens erect, that you cannot really expect to get to 60mph from rest in much less than 25 seconds fully loaded, and that you may get fuel consumption in the order of 30mpg (Imperial). Someone looking to buy a T-Series for the very first time, therefore, must come to terms with the fact that on the trial run he will certainly think he is in rather a small and slow car. After all, the figures quoted can be beaten easily by every modern 1-litre saloon car on the road, and by almost every Austin-Healey Sprite or related MG Midget ever built between 1958 and 1979. The potential T-Series buyer must come to terms with the thought that its charm is not in straight-line performance, but in handling, response and character.

Which type of car should you buy? That really is not for me to recommend. However, it is worth pointing out that there are two distinct types of T-Series, with different characteristics. The TA/TB/TC models are definitely traditional through-and-through, with hard suspension, flexible chassis, few creature comforts, and restricted passenger accommodation. TD/TF models, on the other hand, still look traditional, but have more modern chassis, a much softer ride and suspension, but better and more precise steering. There is more accommodation for people (width in particular) but still precious little stowage space. In no case can you buy a T-Series model in which your valuables are safe, for these cars were never sold with permanently fixed roof panels or glass side windows (except, partly, the TA/TB Tickford).

You will almost certainly get cold in each and every one of the types, and you will always get your signalling arm wet in inclement weather. You will definitely find it difficult to keep up with the faster and more modern sports cars on any but the twistiest of roads, but you will certainly make the journeys with a great deal more style.

The question of spares, maintenace and rebuilding I will leave to the final chapter, but in the case of these cars, which are all quite elderly, you should make a careful inspection before asking for a trial run (you *are* going to insist on a trial run for a car which is not actually in pieces, aren't you?) and there are certain things to look for. If you are buying something which is what my North American friends call a 'parts car' (which means that it is not worth restoring, but may be worth stripping for major

The cylinder-head, combustion chamber and valve layout of the TB/TC Midget – that of the legendary XPAG engine used on all Midgets built from spring 1939 to summer 1955. All derivatives of this engine family, which originated with the Morris 10 Series M car of 1938 (the engine was then coded XPJM for the Morris model) had an overhead-valve layout and there were no compromises necessary to accommodate alternative side-valve layouts.

spares) the following remarks do not apply. Otherwise:

Is the car more or less complete? By this I mean does it have the major and important organs in place? You can certainly find a hood and sidescreens if they are missing, but how difficult will it be to get a missing front wing (fender) or a radiator block?

Is the chassis straight — not distorted in any way? You can usually tell if it is twisted (quite possible on the flimsy TA/TB/TC frame, but not likely on a TD/TF model unless the car has been in a major accident) by a visual inspection, by following the car down the road to watch the attitude of the

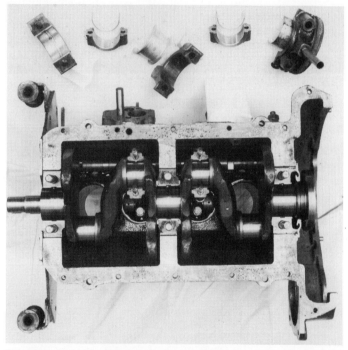

This view of the XPAG's crankcase and crankshaft (this is an early TB engine of 1939 vintage) shows important and obvious philosophical differences compared with the unit used in the TA model. Note the counterbalanced crankshaft and the shell bearings at all bearing surfaces. On the XPAG engine, the crankcase/sump split is at the centreline of the crankshaft drive-line and makes assembly and strip-down that important bit easier.

wheels, and by the feel of the handling on a trial run. If it is bent, you should be chastened by the thought that new chassis are now virtually impossible to find, and that in any case a complete car rebuild would be needed to replace this item.

What is the basic condition of the body? Although, within reason, there is every chance that you could obtain new panels, new sections, or even completely new framework, it is a costly business. All T-Series cars were built on the basis of a wooden (ash) frame with steel panels. The steel panels go rusty (MGs were certainly no better than their rivals in this respect) and the wood rots. A bit of pushing and pulling of doors on hinges, of bonnets on pivots, and of wings on supports will soon tell you a story. A few creaks here and there may not be anything serious to worry about, but badly fitting doors, bonnet panels which open and close with difficulty, and that vague but ominous soggy feeling around the main frames can all be ultimately very discouraging.

Is it original? You will certainly need this book, probably one or other of the specialized service handbooks, and an eagle eye on a hoist to check, but there should be plenty of clues. The right combination of chassis, engine and registration numbers is encouraging for a start (but remember that there are crooks in all forms of business), but is the appropriate type of air-cleaner there, is the colour/trim combination correct, and — very important, this — have any replacement glass-fibre panels been fitted? Delving even deeper, which gearbox and gearbox extension is fitted (the TA/TB/TC box is sometimes completely replaced by the more easily available TD/TF variety, which may be a good short-cut to keeping a car going, but it makes something of a hybrid out of the car) and are you even sure that the correct internal ratios are installed? The supplement to Appendix A shows just how many different sets of ratios have been floating around the MG scene since the mid-1930s; how important is this type of originality to you?

A good chassis inspection is advisable because although the main members will usually have lasted very well, considering the age of the car, there are innumerable 'hang-on' brackets, tubes and other bits and pieces which will have corroded badly and, indeed, may already have been replaced at least once in the life of a particular car. However, the TA/TB/TC chassis is so simple that it can usually be rebuilt (or, to state this more accurately, reconstructed) by a determined mechanic. Quite a lot of wear can occur in moving suspension items, so unless you are being offered an immaculately maintained or restored T-Series model you should expect to find slop in bearings, geometry which is not perfect and steering gear which is not as precise as it might be.

It is essential, therefore, to take a test run (and *not* just a drive round the block) to shake out your possible T-Series purchase *before* you conclude the deal. Many years ago I bought a TA (for £180, in 1959!) on the basis of a very sketchy run and on the assurances of someone I thought I knew well enough. The very first time I drove it at more than 60mph for any length of time one of the engine's big-end bearings collapsed. Then, of course, it was too late, and of course no guarantee had been asked for, or given.

The test run will confirm your hopes (or dash them, perhaps) about the chassis and suspension condition. Make sure that run includes bad roads as well as good, bumpy surfaces as well as motorway-standard conditions, so that you will learn about the integrity and behaviour of the suspension and the state of the steering gear. Make sure that you try the car at most of the speed of which it should be capable, and be sure that the gearbox sounds and feels about right. Remember (yes, I know it is a horrid world) that there are more credulous buyers than sellers. Many cars look and feel acceptable when they are cold, but how do they perform when the drive-line and the engine have thoroughly warmed-up? Be vigilant, for instance, over engine-oil pressure, water temperature (most T-Series engines run rather cool because of the generous size of the water radiator) and oil-tightness. Is that gearbox noise due to noisy gears or a lack of oil? Lastly (and it may not be a major potential expense, but it might immobilize you at an embarrassing moment) check that the battery and dynamo are doing their jobs properly. On the TA and TB the two batteries were hidden in trays on the chassis frame just ahead of the back axle, which is an ideal place for them to be ignored and fall into decline.

This can only be the briefest possible advice on how to assess the T-Series MG sports car you may be thinking of buying, and you have to approach each potential deal on its merits. Ask

As on all the Morris-derived '102 mm stroke' engines built until the late-1930s, the drive was taken through a cork-lined clutch which ran in a bath of oil. This arrangement, illustrated here, was used on the TA Midgets, but replaced for TB and subsequent models by more modern single-dry-plate clutches.

yourself, for instance, not only if you think the price asked is anything like the value you would put on a T-Series, and whether you can face the job of restoring the car to an acceptable state if a poor one is being offered? Of equal importance, in these days when a T-Series car is considered to be an investment, ask yourself why such a fine car is being sold at all, if not for a large profit? Could there be something hidden away behind its attractive lines which is going to cost a fortune to repair, and is the last owner hoping to pass on his problems and heartbreaks to you?

The spares and maintenance problem, however, is not as serious as you might fear, and the last chapter is devoted to this aspect of T-Series ownership.

CHAPTER 9

Maintenance and fellowship

The clubs, the spares and restoration

First the Bad News, and then the Good News. The Bad News is that it is no longer possible to draw on a factory-based stock of spare parts for any T-Series MG. The Good News, however, is that private enterprise in the shape of MG specialists in Britain and North America have ensured that many new spare parts are still being manufactured. It is not easy, and it is certainly not cheap, to maintain and restore a T-Series MG sports car, but it is possible.

The basic problem, of course, is one of passing years. I don't think it is fair to criticize MG (or, more accurately, B.L. Components, the spare-parts division at Cowley) for not holding stocks of spare parts, or even technical literature, for a series of models which went out of production at least 25 years ago. Most firms, as a matter of policy, keep stocks for cars which have become obsolete in the past ten years or so, but within reason British Leyland have tried to extend that 'life' for mechanical spare parts which seem to remain in steady demand. However, when I was preparing an earlier book in this series (*The MGA, MGB and MGC*), I discovered that even the MGA, which was built after the demise of the T-Series models, and which sold to the tune of 101,000 examples in seven years, is virtually no longer covered by the factory. In any case, not for many years has the MG factory held its own stocks, as this operation was rationalized into the Nuffield/B.M.C. system a full generation ago.

British Leyland (or B.M.C. before them) came to terms with this problem in an acceptable way some years ago. Wherever possible it supplied drawings and all related technical details to the MG clubs, or to their approved suppliers, so that duplicate spare parts could be made, or firms which originally supplied MG when the T-Series cars were in production could be encouraged to do so again to the clubs on a more limited scale.

Even the largest MG clubs, however, cannot operate on the same grand scale as they would like, and I have certainly not heard of any MG specialist 'doing a Bugatti' and having major new castings for cylinder-blocks, gearboxes and axle casings made available. This, therefore, is why the stock of T-Series MG cars is slowly and inexorably decreasing. Every time some owner is unlucky enough to suffer frost damage in his engine, or to have a major mechanical disaster connected with motor sports, he becomes more and more desperate in his search for a replacement.

The first point I should cover, therefore, is that of interchangeability with other models. Nowadays, of course, it is not justifiable to suggest that you should try to cannibalize a suitable MG saloon, Morris or Wolseley model for the parts which might suit your T-Series, as the specialist clubs which serve these cars will obviously object violently. However (and this is only likely to apply in Great Britain or perhaps in parts of the old British Empire), you might just find a suitably derelict Morris or Wolseley car which is not worth the trouble of resuscitating.

A general word of warning, however — it is by no means as easy to find *strictly* interchangeable parts in contemporary Morris and Wolseley cars as you might think, as I hope I made clear in earlier chapters. On the other hand, major castings and components from derelict saloons could be very useful to you, such as for the gearbox of a TA or the axle of a TF. There is no space, nor scope, here to delve too deeply into the parts which

118

can fit, and those which might be made to fit, but when you join your appropriate enthusiastic MG club (and you should do so, it is one of the wisest investments any T-Series owner can make) you will probably find that the Spares Secretary has already made something of a study of this. One of the most valuable sources of such information would be the parts book appropriate to your T-Series (which you can buy), accompanied by that of the nearest equivalent Nuffield saloon of the period (which might be difficult to find, especially if you live out of Great Britain).

In general terms (I will not be drawn into the murky depths on the subject of *exact* interchangeability), many of the TA's mechanical fittings were based on the Wolseley 10/40 and 12/48 models of 1936 and 1937, but not as closely on the Series II Morris Tens and Twelves of the same period. The Series III Morris and Wolseley models which took over for 1938 (and were built until 1948) could also be a useful source.

TC/TD/TF1250 engines shared some, but by no means all, parts, (the basic cylinder-block, for instance, had different cylinder-bore dimensions) with the Morris Ten Series M/Wolseley Ten of 1939 to 1948, but there was much more commonization with the YA/YB/YT family of MGs built between 1947 and 1953. It would surely be wrong, however, to advocate scrapping a Y-Type MG to keep a T-Series sports car on the road?

A surprisingly promising source of engine and gearbox parts might be the Wolseley 4/44 announced in 1952 (which had a single-carburettor derivative of the XP . . engine family), though there is nothing to be gained by looking at the MG Magnette announced in 1953 as it had the B.M.C. B-Series engine and transmission used later on the MGA.

Many proprietary items, too, like brake and clutch fittings, were virtually standard items for their day, and after consulting your club specialists, or perhaps your specialist supplier, you might find alternative sources of parts. It costs nothing to ask, and one is often pleased with a discovery, but a really well-established club will have explored most such avenues, so don't expect miracles.

The situation regarding chassis frames is that new ones are not available, nor has any enterprizing *entrepreneur* taken the deep breath and enormous financial gamble necessary to arrange for new frames to be made. Both types of frame, however — TA/TB/TC and TD/TF — are relatively simple, and I have no doubt that some restorers are skilful enough to manufacture completely new sections to repair or restore rusting old frames. Unless you are a *concours* 'buff', and cannot face the thought of a chopped and buttressed frame (because it would penalize you against a more original specimen), this may be one solution to your problem.

The TA/TB/TC frame has absolutely no near-relatives among other Nuffield cars; Morris and Wolseley models of the period had nothing in common with it, and the contemporary MGs (SA/VA/WA) used entirely different pressings. The TD/TF frame, of course, was originally derived from that of the YA/YB/YT MG models, but in production form they had little in common apart from the front suspension and cross-member and a few brackets; the Y-type frame had a longer wheelbase, mounted an entirely different type of body, and the main box-section side-members ran under the back axle, rather than over it like the TD's frame. Not even the YA/YT axle is common with that of the TD, though the YB of 1951 to 1953 was converted to the hypoid axle, wheels, tyres and brakes of the same dimensions as a TD; however, the YB did not have perforated disc wheels.

Unloved T-Series bodies had a poor reputation, because they deteriorated rather rapidly unless the cars lived in a very dry climate. Built by the Morris Bodies Branch in Coventry, they suffered from every malady known to a coachbuilt shell — the steel panels soon began to rust away, the wooden shell was not too rigid when new and even less so when old, and the wood itself became fragile and crumbled away with one of several types of rot. It is not only in private houses than the phenomenon of dry and wet rot appears!

Fortunately it is now possible to repair, restore, or completely replace the bodywork of a T-Series MG, as specialists have reconstructed their own jigs and formers to allow anything from a bonnet panel to a swept wing, a facia to a complete body frame, to be produced. Furthermore, these modern wooden-framed bodies are better built and use modern preservatives, so you should be able to justify some of the admittedly high cost of rebodying your car with the thought that it might last rather longer than did the original. But do not fall into the trap of buying glass-fibre panels, as you will always be the object of scorn from fellow MG enthusiasts. (It falls into the same category as those misguided individuals who buy a MG 'replica' on a Triumph chassis!)

Fittings, too, for T-Series MG bodies, such as hoods, side-screens, trim and floors, can all be found, and your club will usually be able to tell you which is the nearest, most reliable, or most professional supplier of such new items. It is usually necessary to have poor chrome replated, and to have faulty instruments rebuilt, while a major disaster as far as any MG enthusiast is concerned is that a faulty radiator will certainly have to be rebuilt, not replaced, at considerable cost. Seats can be retrimmed, usually with authentic and near-accurate materials.

The clubs, particularly in countries other than Great Britain and the United States, are vital to this rebuilding and restoration business. There are MG clubs in most countries where there are MGs; some concentrate on the sport of motoring and on the social side, while others are much more concerned with the location, initiation and supply of new spare parts and technical information.

The two major MG clubs, both British-based, are the MG Car Club Ltd, and the MG Owners' Club. The 'Car Club' is the oldest, and was once factory-based, while the 'Owners' Club' is the largest, and in fact now claims to be the largest one-make club in Great Britain, with which nobody seems to be arguing. A smaller, but nevertheless enthusiastic club, which caters for all pre-1956 MGs, and draws almost all its members from Great Britain, is the Octagon Car Club.

The MG Car Club was founded in 1930, and had John Thornley as its original organizing secretary. Thornley joined MG towards the end of 1931, where his main job was to run the MG Car Club, but he also had to assist the service manager at the plant. Within a year or so he became service manager, but still kept his function in the Car Club until his place was taken by Alan Hess.

As long as John Thornley was at Abingdon (he ran the factory until after the British Leyland takeover), the MG Car Club had official factory approval and support, and it was only in 1969 that it had to take on a separate existence after financial help and office space at Abingdon was withdrawn. The club, which has been a Limited Company since then, also took over the title of the famous MG magazine *Safety Fast*.

The MG Car Club caters for every type of MG, and a good proportion of its members worldwide have T-Series models. Membership of the club, incidentally, is confined not to MG owners, but to MG enthusiasts. When this book went to press at the beginning of 1980 there were about 5,500 British members, and nearly 10,000 more members in the various overseas sections. Unlike the other major club, the Car Club's activities are principally competitive (which means that anything from a full-blooded race meeting to a local driving test or trial might be involved), with over 1,000 events of all types taking place, worldwide, each year.

The club has sections, or centres, all over the world. In Britain there are eight separate Registers, of which the T-Series Register is obviously the one most important to readers of this book. The following contacts, which are correct as of January 1980, will therefore be of value:

Gordon Cobban,
General Secretary, MG Car Club Ltd.,
P.O. Box 126,
Brentwood,
Essex CM15 8RP.

However, for all matters regarding membership, you should contact:

Sheila Laurence,
Registration Secretary,
67 Wide Bargate,
Barston,
Lincolnshire PE21 6LE.

Many T-Series owners and enthusiasts live in North America, and should know that the activities of the MG Car Club in their continent are co-ordinated by British Leyland from their headquarters near New York. There are about 30 different MG Car Club centres in North America, and for details about them (and for up-to-date information about contact addresses) you should get in touch with:

Fred S. Horner,
MG Car Club,

P.O. Box 423,
Locust Valley,
NY 11560.
USA.

Here in Britain, the T-Series Register is thriving, and apart from the racing activities of its members, it is also much involved in maintenance and restoration of the type. As this book closes for press I hear that the Register is preparing a vast and detailed tome about the maintenance and modification of all the T-Series machines, which eventually they hope to publish in book form. The Secretary of the T-Series Register is:

Glyn Giusti,
57 Norman Crescent,
Pinner,
Middlesex.

It is worth pointing out that not only is the MG Car Club very active in Great Britain and in North America, but it also has thriving branches in most European countries, Japan, Africa, Australia and New Zealand. The publication *Safety Fast*, which is circulated free to all members, keeps the whole organization in touch with every other part and regularly publishes lists of contacts for each country.

When I was writing my earlier MG Collector's Guide *MGA, MGB and MGC*, the Car Club told me that they had set up a new company — CK Spares Ltd — to look into the manufacture of new spare parts from official factory blueprints and specifications supplied to them from time to time by British Leyland as those parts become officially obsolete and out of stock.

Safety Fast, too, contains advertisements from various MG parts and restoration specialists, all of whom have been checked out and approved by the Club before it accepts their business. It follows that a company whose name and products appear in *Safety Fast* is one of which Car Club members know and approve, and while it does *not* follow that a company which is unapproved by the Club may be below standard, such omissions do sometimes tell a story!

The other large MG club, the MG Owners' Club, is still almost entirely British-based, though this situation may change

in the next few years. In Britain, with nearly 16,000 members (16,000 is no misprint) it dwarfs the Car Club, but does not duplicate its efforts as it performs different functions. The MG Owners' Club, which looks after the interests of any MG owner and enthusiast, was only founded in 1973, yet membership passed the 5,000 mark within five years and has mushroomed rapidly in the last two years. It caters mainly for the owners of MGs and Austin-Healeys built since the demise of the T-Series Midgets, but more and more new members have T-Series cars, and there is a steady build-up of knowledge and expertize in the Club about these fine models.

The MG Owners' Club places its emphasis of service on the supply of parts, technical advice and literature, and is now looking more and more at the reprinting of literature connected with MGs which has long since gone out of print from British Leyland.

The General Secretary is:

Roche Bentley,
The MG Owners' Club,
13 Church End,
Over,
Cambridgeshire CB4 5NH.

Within the club there are spares secretaries for each type of MG, and there is a permanently staffed headquarters at Over (Tel: 0954-31172) to deal with all queries. The Club's magazine is *Enjoying MG*, published regularly, in which there is a constant flow of information about restoration, maintenance, the situation regarding spare parts and technical information supplies, along with hints and tips about the cars from club members with personal experience.

The third significant club, formed as a breakaway from the MG Car Club in 1969, is the Octagon Car Club, which caters specifically for owners of older MGs and is not diverted by matters referring to MGAs, MGBs and MGCs. This means that it is a particularly appropriate club for T-Series owners to join; the membership roll proves this, as at the beginning of 1980 about 400 of the 700 club members owned T-Series models. The Octagon Car Club's aims are all-embracing, with activities ranging from sport to social events, with a regular club publication and information on spares and technical matters. The secretary of the Octagon Car Club is:

Harry Crutchley,
Octagon Car Club,
36 Queensville Avenue,
Stafford,
Staffordshire.

I do not propose to quote membership and election fees to any of these clubs as they differ from country to country, while I am sure I do not have to labour the point that inflation (in almost every country) makes regular increases in charges necessary. From my own experience, however, I would suggest that the MG Car Club is most noted for its sport, the Owners' Club for its technical know-how, and the Octagon Club for its enthusiasm particularly for the T-Series cars. If you live outside Great Britain or Western Europe the Car Club is the most obvious candidate for your membership.

In this way, of course, you will be able to enjoy ownership of your T-Series MG sports car to the highest degree, which is surely what MG ownership should be all about? I hope that in writing this book I have not encouraged too many people to 'take the *concours* trail', or to see their cars merely as beautiful objects rather than as working machines. Indeed, I hope that two of the club magazines' titles tell their own story about these fine cars—that *Enjoying MG* is what T-Series ownership should be all about, and that all your motoring, therefore, should be *Safety Fast*.

APPENDIX A

Technical specifications of all T-Series MGs

TA model — produced 1936 to 1939
Engine: 4-cyl, 63.5 × 102mm, 1,292cc, CR 6.5:1, 2 SU carbs, valve operation by pushrods and rockers. 50bhp at 4,500rpm. Maximum torque not quoted.
Transmission: Axle ratio 4.875:1, spiral-bevel gears. Overall gear ratios (first 183 cars, to Engine No MPJG 683) 4.875, 6.92, 10.73, 18.11, reverse 23.26:1, without synchromesh; (from Engine No MPJG 684) 4.875, 6.44, 9.95, 16.84, reverse 21.64:1, with synchromesh on top and third gears. 16.64mph/1,000rpm in top gear.
Suspension and brakes: Beam front axle, half-elliptic leaf springs, Luvax hydraulic lever-arm dampers; live rear axle, half-elliptic leaf springs, Luvax hydraulic lever-arm dampers. Cam-gear steering. 9 × 1.5in front and rear drum brakes, hydraulically operated. 4.50-19in tyres on 2.5in rims. Centre-lock wire-spoke wheels.
Dimensions: Wheelbase 7ft 10in; front track 3ft 9in; rear track 3ft 9in. Length 11ft 7.5in; width 4ft 8in; height 4ft 5in (with hood erect). Unladen weight 1,765lb.
Basic Price: £222 (2-seater), £269.50 (Tickford-bodied 2-seater coupe).

TB model — produced in 1939
Specifications as for TA except for:
Engine: 66.5 × 90mm, 1,250cc, CR 7.25:1, 54bhp at 5,200rpm; maximum torque 64lb ft at 2,600rpm.
Transmission: Axle ratio 5.125:1, spiral-bevel gears. Overall gear ratios 5.125, 6.92, 10.0 17.32, reverse 17.32:1. 15.84mph/1,000rpm in top gear.
Basic price: £225 (2-seater), £270 (Tickford-bodied 2-seater coupe).

TC model — produced 1945 to 1949
Specification as for TA except for:
Engine: 66.5 × 90mm, 1,250cc, CR 7.25:1, 54bhp at 5,200rpm; maximum torque 64lb ft at 2,600rpm.
Transmission: Axle ratio 5.125:1, spiral-bevel gears. Overall gear ratios 5.125, 6.92, 10.0, 17.32, reverse 17.32:1. 15.84mph/1,000rpm in top gear. Unladen weight 1,735lb.
Basic price: £375 in 1945, £412.50 from mid-1946. In the USA, $2,238 in 1948, $2,395 in 1949.

TD model — produced 1950 to 1953
Engine: 4-cyl, 66.5 × 90mm, 1,250cc. CR 7.25:1, 54bhp at 5,200rpm; maximum torque 64lb ft at 2,600rpm.
Transmission: Axle ratio 5.125:1, hypoid-bevel gears. Overall gear ratios 5.125, 7.098, 10.609, 17.938, reverse 17.938:1. 14.4mph/1,000rpm in top gear.
Suspension and brakes: Ifs, coil springs, wishbones, hydraulic lever-arm dampers; live rear axle, half-elliptic leaf springs, hydraulic lever-arm dampers. Rack-and-pinion steering. 9 × 1.5in front and rear drum brakes. 5.50-15in tyres on 4.0in rims. Steel disc wheels only at first; optional centre-lock wire-spoke wheels introduced later.
Dimensions: Wheelbase 7ft 10in; front track 3ft 11.4in; rear track 4ft 2in. Length 12ft 1in; width 4ft 10.6in; height (hood erect) 4ft 5in. Unladen weight 1,930lb.
Basic price: £445 on announcement, £470 from April 1951, £530 from autumn 1952. In the USA, $1,850 in 1950, $1,975 in 1951, $2,115 in 1952 and 1953, $2,145 (for old stock) in 1954.

TD II Model — produced to special order, 1951 to 1953
Specification as for TD model except for:
Engine: CR 8.0:1, 60bhp at 5,500rpm. Overall gear ratios 4.875, 6.75, 10.10, 17.08, reverse 17.08:1. 15.2mph/1,000rpm in top gear.
Basic price: (USA) $2,210 in 1951, $2,360 in 1952 and 1953.

TF1250 model — produced 1953 and 1954
Engine: 66.5 × 90mm, 1,250cc. CR 8.0:1, 57bhp at 5,500rpm; maximum torque 65lb ft at 3,000rpm.
Transmission: Axle ratio 4.875:1, hypoid-bevel gears. Overall gear ratios 4.875, 6.752, 10.09, 17.06, reverse 17.06:1. 15.25mph/1,000rpm in top gear.
Suspension and brakes: Ifs, coil springs, wishbones, hydraulic lever-arm dampers; live rear axle, half-elliptic leaf spring, hydraulic lever-arm dampers. Rack-and-pinion steering. 9 × 1.5in front and rear drum brakes. 5.50-15in tyres on 4.0in rims. Steel disc or centre-lock wire-spoke wheels.
Dimensions: Wheelbase 7ft 10in; front track 3ft 11.4in; rear track 4ft 2in. Length 12ft 3in; width 4ft 11.7in; height (hood erect) 4ft 4.5in. Unladen weight 1,930lb.
Basic price: £550. In the USA, $2,250.

TF1500 model — produced 1954 and 1955

Specification as for TF1250 except for:
Engine: 72 × 90mm, 1,466cc. CR 8.3:1. 63bhp at 5,000rpm; maximum torque 76lb ft at 3,000 rpm.
Basic price: (USA) $1,995.

Supplement: T-Series and closely related gearboxes

From 1936 to 1939 several different types of gearbox, and different ratios, were used on T-Types and related models in the Nuffield Group, all using the same cast-iron case. For interest, and in case anyone restoring a T-Series car has any illusions about the degree of standardization between related models, the sets of appropriate *internal* gearbox ratios are below:

Model	Internal ratios	Comments
TA	1.00, 1.42, 2.20, 3.715, reverse 4.78:1	No synchromesh, used up to Engine No MPJG 683.
TA	1.00, 1.32, 2.04, 3.454, reverse 4.44:1	Synchromesh on top and third gears, used from Engine No MPJG 684.
TB	1.00, 1.35, 1.95, 3.38, reverse 3.38:1	Synchromesh on top, third and second gears.
TC	1.00, 1.35, 1.95, 3.38, reverse 3.38:1	Exactly as for TB, with synchromesh on top, third and second gears.
TD	1.00, 1.385, 2.07, 3.50, reverse 3.50:1	Synchromesh on top, third and second gears. New gear box extension.
TF	1.00, 1.385, 2.07, 3.50, reverse 3.50:1	Exactly as for TD.

Related gearboxes

Model	Internal ratios	Comments
SA	1.00, 1.38, 2.13, 3.76, reverse 4.76:1	No synchromesh at first, later with synchromesh on top and third gears. Basically of TA type.
VA	1.00, 1.35, 1.95, 3.38, reverse 3.38:1	Same basic gearbox as TB/TC type, with synchromesh on top, third and second gears.
WA	1.00, 1.418, 2.155, 3.646, reverse 3.646:1	Synchromesh on top, third and second gears. TB/TC type of box but different ratios.
YA/YB/YT	1.00, 1.385, 2.07, 3.50, reverse 3.50:1	Box as TD/TF, but with different gear-selection arrangements.

Various Morris and Wolseley models built between 1936 and 1948 used the same basic gearbox casing and some common components, but invariably used different sets of ratios. These cars also used direct-action gear-changes, or semi-remote-control changes like those found on Y-Series models. The box fitted to the Wolseley 4/44, which used a Y-Type 1,250cc engine, was a wide-ratio variety converted to steering-column gear-change. The box fitted to the MG Magnette announced in 1953 was an entirely different B.M.C. type.

APPENDIX B

Chassis Number sequences —.by model and date

Model	Years built	Engine	Chassis Nos
TA	June 1936–April 1939	1,292cc	TA0251–3253
TB	May 1939–Sept 1939	1,250cc	TB0251–0629
TC	Nov 1945–Nov 1949	1,250cc	TC0251–10252*
TD I	Nov 1949–Aug 1951	1,250cc	TD0251–9158*
TD II	Aug 1951–Sept 1953	1,250cc	TD9159–29915*
TF1250	Oct 1953–Nov 1954	1,250cc	TF0501–6500, 6651–6750 and 6851–6950
TF1500	Nov 1954–May 1955	1,466cc	TF6501–6650, 6751–6850 and 6951–10100

Note: For many years it was traditional for MG Chassis Number sequences to start from . . . 251 as this was the MG factory's Abingdon telephone number! The TF model, however, did not conform to this sequence; by this time the MG concern was becoming dominated by the influence of the new British Motor Corporation, who decided, in their wisdom, that a start from . . .501 was more seemly. In this, as in so many little details, they showed a complete and unnecessary disregard for historical niceties.

Towards the end of 1954 there was a gradual change-over of production from the TF1250 to TF1500 models, during which batches of each model were built. This explains the intermingling of Chassis Numbers between 6501 and 6950, and potential buyers of TFs built around this time should check the car's Chassis Number very carefully indeed.

*Eagle-eyed mathematicians will already have noted that in the case of the TC and TD models there is a minor, but irritating, discrepancy between the total number of chassis identifications quoted, and the official total of cars built. In the case of the TC the Chassis Number sequence suggests that 10,002 cars were built, while the official total is 10,000. In the case of the TD the Chassis Number sequence suggests the assembly of 29,665 cars, while the official total is 29,664.

In this way, as in others, MG are as enigmatic as other sportscar manufacturers in Britain or the rest of Europe. Both sets of figures, we are assured, are correct. In the case of the TC, however, the author has seen other sources (including the comment of Cecil Cousins) that the first Chassis Number of the TC sequence only applied to the *prototype*, that the first true production car was TC0252 and the last number was in fact TC10251. Final verification, it seems, cannot be made.

The TD total, too, differs by one car only, and one is tempted to suggest that the same explanation will suffice.

TB, TB and TF figures, on the other hand, all correlate exactly with official production figures.

APPENDIX C

MG production and deliveries —.1936 to 1955

A great deal of effort by Jaguar-Rover-Triumph's public relations staff, and by Barry Crook's production control department at Abingdon, has gone into the preparation of the following charts, and I am deeply grateful for their patient help.

Here, perhaps for the first time, it has been possible to show the year-on-year, model-by-model, home-and-export performance of all the T-Series and MG Midgets; however, detail figures for the TA/TB models are no longer available, and in the case of the TA I have had to make what I hope are inspired guesses at the probable sequence of events.

I should emphasize that these figures are for calendar years, and that year-on-year figures refer to production, not to deliveries. As an example, only 1,460 TF1500s are shown as being produced in 1955, which is correct, but due to the 'pipeline' which exists in terms of shipping delays and dealer stocks, rather more than that number were registered and delivered during the year. Similarly, no MG TD was actually sold to its owner before January 1950, even though the first 98 production cars were built before the end of 1949; MG TCs, certainly, were still being registered in certain export markets in the first months of 1950.

Details production figures turn up many interesting details:

(a) The TC's peak year was 1948, though it is likely that even more cars would have been built in 1949 if the model had been continued. The best export year for the TC, in any case, was 1949.

(b) The TD's peak came in 1952, with more than 10,800 cars built. In that year, as many TDs were built as the total production of TCs in four years, and almost as many as the combined total of M-Type, J2, PA, PB, TA and TB production between 1929 and 1939.

(c) There was a fall of production in 1953 compared with the peak year of 1952, but this had as much to do with the phasing-in of two new models — TF in place of TD, ZA Magnette in place of YB 1¼-litre — as to a lowering of demand.

(d) The myth of TC exports to the USA has been well-and-truly exploded. First TC export did not begin until 1947 and a total of 2,001 TCs (20 per cent of the total production) were sold in the USA. The *real* export success for Abingdon was the TD.

(e) USA exports hit a peak in 1952 and declined dramatically thereafter. From 9,901 Abingdon exports in 1952, the total slumped to a mere 1,288 three years later — a sure sign that the TF Midget was not what the United States market wanted. The leeway was taken up, to sighs of gratitude, by British customers, who took as many new MGs as they could.

(f) It is amazing what variety of cars Abingdon could assemble, as one of the charts shows clearly. In 1950, for instance, Abingdon assembly lines were producing TD Midgets, YA 1¼-litre saloons, YT Tourers, Riley RMA 1½-litre saloons, Riley RMB saloons, tourers and coupes. In 1955, too, they excelled themselves, building substantial quantities of TF1500s, MGAs, ZA and ZB Magnettes, Riley RME 1½-litre saloons and Riley Pathfinders.

(g) MG enthusiasts should realize that well over half the total of all T-Series Midgets built were exported to the United States. When new, however, no TAs or TBs were sold in the United States, and very few were exported elsewhere.

(h) It is interesting to realize that more TCs were delivered in Britain than TDs, both in absolute terms (3,408 compared with 1,656) and in percentage terms (34 compared with 5 per cent — and 13 per cent of the TFs); so where have they all gone?

T-Series MG production figures — 1936 to 1955

Calendar year	TA Midget	TB Midget	TC Midget	TD Midget	TF Midget
1936	500*				
1937	1,100*				
1938	900*				
1939	500*	379			
— —	break in production due to World War Two			— —	
1945			81		
1946			1,675		
1947			2,346		
1948			3,085		
1949			2,813	98	
1950				4,767	
1951				7,451	
1952				10,838	
1953				6,510	1,620
1954					6,520
1955					1,460†
Total	3,003	379	10,000	29,664	9,600

* No exact figures are available. These, therefore, are estimates based on MG's total production performance, the phase-in and phase-out dates of the TA model and — frankly — inspired guesswork.

† Production of the TF ran out in May 1955. MGA production began in August 1955, and 1,003 examples were built before the end of the year. 1955, therefore, was the least-productive year for sports cars at Abingdon since 1947 and was the first year in which there has ever been a significant hiatus between the dropping of one model and the start-up of production of the next.

Total deliveries

Model	Year built	Home market	Export — USA	Export — other	CKD*	Total
TA	1936–39		not known			3,003
TB	1939		not known			379
TC	1945–49	3,408	2,001	4,497	94	10,000
TD	1949–53	1,656	23,488	3,911	609	29,664
TF	1953–55	1,242	6,272	1,999	87	9,600
Total	1945–55	6,306	31,761	10,407	790	52,646

* Completely Knocked Down — for assembly in certain export territories.

Other cars built at Abingdon — 1936 to 1955 inclusive

While the T-Series MG sports cars were in production at Abingdon, considerable numbers of other MG and Riley models were being assembled on parallel lines. Postwar production of MG saloons, starting with the YA 1¼-litre model, began in 1947, while Riley assembly was transferred from Coventry to Abingdon in 1949.

In the case of overlapping models like the RM Rileys, the Riley Pathfinder and the ZA Magnette, it has not been possible to ascertain exactly how many of each model were built before TF production ceased. In each case, therefore, a production total to the end of 1955 has been quoted. These were:

Make and Model	Year built	Quantity produced
SA model (2.3-litre)	1936–39	2,738
VA model (1½-litre)	1937–39	2,407
WA model (2.6-litre)	1938–39	369
— — break in production due to World War Two — —		
YA saloon (1¼-litre)	1947–51	6,158
YT tourer (1¼-litre)	1948–50	877
YB saloon (1¼-litre)	1951–53	1,301
ZA Magnette saloon (1½-litre)	1953–55	12,754

Riley RMA saloons (1½-litre)	1949–53	5,479
Riley RMB/RMF saloons (2½-litre)	1949–53	5,639
Riley RME saloons (1½-litre)	1953–55	2,096
Riley RMB roadster (2½-litre)	1949–51	386
Riley RMB coupe (2½-litre)	1949–51	498
Riley Pathfinder saloon (2½-litre)	1954–55	3,608

Total Abingdon production — 1945 to 1955 inclusive

The chart printed below shows how Abingdon's *total* production built up impressively between 1945 and 1952, but stabilized for the next three years. These figures include production of other MG and Riley models, including (in 1955) the first 1,003 MGA sports cars.

Calendar year	Home market	General export	USA market	CKD*	Total
1945	34	47	—	—	81
1946	1,001	638	—	36	1,675
1947	1,591	1,656	6	16	3,269
1948	584	1,985	1,493	114	4,176
1949	2,421	3,800	662	163	7,046
1950	2,630	4,429	2,825	546	10,430
1951	2,369	2,741	5,757	198	11,065
1952	2,575	1,108	9,901	85	13,669
1953	3,012	1,020	6,400	107	10,539
1954	5,276	3,326	4,218	155	12,975
1955	7,697	4,908	1,288	245	14,138

* Completely Knocked Down — for assembly in certain export territories.

APPENDIX D

How fast? How economical? How heavy?

An awful lot of nonsense is often talked about a particular car's performance, and it is fair to suggest that no owner, or car maker, ever underestimates a model's accelerative ability, top speed or fuel economy possibilities. The figures published here, however sketchy and at times contradictory, have been recorded by reputable motoring magazines, on standard cars provided for the purpose either by the MG factory itself, or by their representatives in North America. They may be considered to be fully representative of the current T-Series model in good and as-new condition.

Perhaps because they were never very happy with the somewhat limited performance of their T-Series cars, MG were not too generous with the loan of cars to the British press; this attitude was certainly a hangover from the end of the 1930s when MG withdrew almost all test-car facilities after their own accusations of cheating against other manufacturers had been discovered to be without foundation.

No TF model was ever loaned to a British magazine for performance figures to be recorded, either in 1,250cc or in 1,466cc form. For that reason, the TDII, TD Mark 2, TF1250 and TF1500 figures quoted are those recorded by *Road and Track* magazine in the United States, while those for the TA, TC and the original TD are from that most authoritative of British magazines *The Autocar*. Although *The Motor*'s figures were often slightly better, they were achieved in those years without the aid of a fifth-wheel speedometer and consequently have been questioned by some neutral observers.

Several British magazines drove TB models, but none was apparently allowed to take performance figures, but one might assume that the TB's performance must have been closely comparable to that of the postwar TC model.

There are serious discrepancies between the general level of performance achieved by *The Autocar* and *Road and Track*, which can only satisfactorily be explained by the different methods used. *The Autocar* habitually tested their cars with driver and passenger, and recorded speeds on a fifth-wheel speedometer. The acceleration figures recorded by *Road and Track* are better than the British figures (with engines of similar horsepower), yet two people were also carried, and I suspect the 'corrected-speedometer' method of timing was used, which has now been shown to be rather less accurate.

The lessons to be learned from these test figures, British or American, are the T-Series MGs all suffered badly from their poor aerodynamic qualities, which affected high-speed acceleration, top speed and potential fuel economy. It is instructive to compare a TF1500's performance with that of a 1956 model MGA 1500 which replaced it. The latter model had perhaps five to eight brake horsepower more, and weighed slightly less, yet its maximum speed was at least 13mph better, due mostly to the smooth fully-streamlined shape, and it was also significantly more economical in its use of fuel.

Between 1936 and 1955 the weight of standard production T-Series MGs rose by only 100lb according to the published figures (but by 165lb according to factory figures), which is most creditable when the increased bulk of the TF, and its more comprehensive equipment, is considered in relation to the TA.

The TD and TF models had lower overall gearing than the TA had back in 1936 (in other words, the engine had to rev faster to produce the same road speed) which is one indication of the way MG tried to regain greater acceleration for their later models without resorting to more highly tuned engines; the performance figures indicate that this had to be bought at the expense of an increase in fuel consumption. The MGA of 1955, which replaced the TF1500, was considerably higher-geared, and was rather more economical in spite of having a more powerful engine.

In outright terms, there is not a great deal of difference between the performance of TC, TD and TF models when fitted with the same type of 1¼-litre XPAG engine. The TA, when current, clearly had less power and torque than its successors, but one wonders how much quicker a TA might have been if tested with the higher-grade fuel available for the TDs and TFs of the 1950s?

	TA 1,292 cc	TC 1,250 cc	TD 1,250 cc	TD II 1,250 cc	TD Mark 2 1,250 cc	TF1250 1,250 cc	TF1500 1,466 cc
Mean maximum speed (mph)	78	75	80	79	81	80	85
Acceleration (sec)							
0–30mph	6.1	5.7	6.2	5.2	5.2	5.5	4.8
0–40mph	—	—	—	8.8	7.5	8.8	7.1
0–50mph	15.4	14.7	15.3	13.8	11.1	13.0	11.0
0–60mph	23.1	22.7	23.5	19.4	16.5	18.9	16.3
0–70mph	—	—	44.4	31.8	24.4	29.0	24.7
Standing ¼-mile (sec)	—	—	—	21.3	20.8	21.6	20.7
Top gear (sec)							
10–30mph	13.2	12.1	12.5	—	—	—	—
20–40mph	15.2	13.5	12.2	—	—	—	—
30–50mph	17.2	14.9	12.9	—	—	—	—
Overall fuel consumption (mpg)	—	—	—	24.3*	21.9*	20/23*	—
Typical fuel consumption (mpg)	27/29	28/34	27/33	—	—	—	—
Kerb weight (lb)	1,935	1,811	2,009	2,005	2,015	2,020	2,015
Original test published	1936	1947	1950	1953	1953	1953	1954

*US gallons

Note: TD II, TD Mark 2 and both TF tests are from *Road and Track* while earlier tests are by courtesy of *The Autocar*.